"This book is a tripartite creation: portrait, self-portrait, and homage, and it draws heavily on the author's much-practiced and celebrated skill as a radio documentarian. The chorus of voices, the leitmotifs, the rich allusions to music, the culminating crescendo of biography mixed imaginatively with autobiography—it's all nicely constructed. Burns rightly locates the Nouwen charisma in his capacious generosity for friendship, in his restless yearning for Love's affirmation. This is the *essential* Nouwen."

—MICHAEL W. HIGGINS, biographer of Henri Nouwen, professor of religious studies and vice-president for mission and Catholic identity, Sacred Heart University, Fairfield, Connecticut

"Kevin Burns's biography of Henri Nouwen is as far-reaching and engaging as his subject. By listening to those who knew one of the greatest modern spiritual writers well, [Burns] has skillfully pieced together insights filtered through the memories of a diverse range of sources. The result is a concise, stimulating exploration of Nouwen the priest-psychologist-professor, and of the interplay among his experience, spiritual development, and hugely influential writings. Though manifestly personally touched, Burns steps back and allows Nouwen to emerge as a restless, uncertain, gifted, supremely human saint in the making, seeking an experience of love and home."

—KATHRYN SPINK, author, *Mother Teresa: An Authorized Biography* and *The Miracle, the Message, the Story: Jean Vanier and L'Arche*

"The life of Henri Nouwen was filled with a fascinating combination of intellectual brilliance coupled with a deep desire to dwell with simplicity. The complexities of his life and the deep tension between sadness and joy that marked his spirituality are not easy to capture or to understand. In this thoughtful and sensitive book, Kevin Burns takes us on a journey that captures some of the spiritual nuances of Nouwen's life and draws out how and why his work continues to be fruitful for the everyday spirituality of many people today. Anyone serious about seeking to understand Nouwen should read this book."

—JOHN SWINTON, chair in divinity and religious studies,
University of Aberdeen, author, *Raging with Compassion*

Henri Nouwen

His Life and Spirit

Kevin Burns

Franciscan
MEDIA
Cincinnati, Ohio

The permissions beginning on page 138 constitute an extension of this copyright page.

Cover and book design by Mark Sullivan
Cover photograph by Neal McDonough. Used with permission of the Henri J.M. Nouwen Archives and Research Collection, John M. Kelly Library, University of Toronto.

Library of Congress Cataloging-in-Publication Data
Names: Burns, Kevin, 1952- author.
Title: Henri Nouwen : his life and spirit / Kevin Burns.
Description: Cincinnati : Franciscan Media, 2016. | Includes bibliographical references.
Identifiers: LCCN 2016022193 | ISBN 9781632531384 (hard cover with dust jacket)
Subjects: LCSH: Nouwen, Henri J. M.
Classification: LCC BX4705.N87 B87 2016 | DDC 282.092 [B] —dc23
LC record available at https://lccn.loc.gov/2016022193
ISBN 978-1-63253-138-4

Published by Franciscan Media
28 W. Liberty St.
Cincinnati, OH 45202
www.FranciscanMedia.org

Printed in the United States of America
Printed on acid-free paper
16 17 18 19 20 5 4 3 2 1

We know little or nothing of our heart. We keep our distance from it as though we are afraid of it. What is most intimate is also what frightens us most. Where we are most ourselves, we are often strangers to ourselves. That is the painful part of our being human. We fail to know our hidden center and so we live and die often without knowing who we really are. If we ask ourselves why we think, feel, and act in a certain way, we often have no answer, thus proving to be strangers in our own house.

—Henri Nouwen[1]

In memory of Fr. James Francis Webb (1935–2013), chaplain of my high school, Blessed (now Saint) Richard Gwyn School, in Flint, North Wales. He was a working-class kid from Britain's tough northeast who scraped his way to Cambridge University— and ordination. For five memorable years, he instilled a sense of inquiry and the belief that anything was possible if we worked for it. He was the first priest with whom I had a meaningful conversation. Too young to realize at the time, I see now a mentor who pointed me in a direction that, decades later, has made this project possible.

And of course, for the beloved B.
Always.

CONTENTS

About Biography

Conversing with Our Friends—the Dead

Did anyone really know Henri Nouwen? His students thought they did. His colleagues thought so. Those who saw him give presentations know what they saw: a tall, physically awkward yet highly animated performer, his unkempt hair all over the place, arms flapping as his hands gestured outwards and upwards. Such energy! Others remember something else, the anguished, prostrated, silent man they saw deep in prayer. His readers certainly believe they know him, as every reader thinks they know the writers they read. When we read an author's work, we befriend them and are confident that we know them intimately and in ways that no one else could possibly understand. We say, sometimes silently, "It doesn't matter what you think, I know how this particular author speaks to me, and that's all that matters." In this, we are creating the author that we are befriending. It's easy when that author shares personal matters, whether in fiction or not.

After years of nonfiction publishing, Henri thought about creating hybrid works that mixed different forms of writing. Although many of his books are based on his journals, they offer relatively brief glimpses into his life, despite his personal, direct, and intimate tone. To read Henri is to discover an uncertain pilgrim on the prowl, hungry for a sense of the experience of home. He's frequently anguished, and he's always in need of reassurance. His successes hide the shadows of deeply felt vulnerability, that nagging uncertainty about feeling loved. Whenever Henri makes a discovery, it takes the form of a great life-changing and life-settling moment—though not always a permanent one. And in that, Henri becomes so wonderfully and recognizably human.

The challenge for any biographer is how to paint such a profoundly elusive human chameleon. As Henri's biographer, I began by scooping up the fragmented details I could glean by talking to people who knew him, either through their direct contact with him or with his work. All biography is like that, built through conversation.

It's the same when we read one. To read a biography is to have a conversation with our friends: the dead. That is how the British biographer Michael Holroyd describes the collaboration between the reader, the writer, and the subject of a biography.[1] The novelist Julian Barnes knows that these conversations are often based on flimsy information. In his playful novel about the challenges of writing a biography of the elusive French author Gustave Flaubert, Barnes says that biographies are filled with details that just happen to get caught in a net that is "a collection of holes tied together with strings." Once that imprecise net is pulled out of the water the biographer "sorts, throws back, stores, fillets, and sells." Barnes asks the reader to consider what the biographer doesn't catch because "there is always more of that."[2] When the biographer Janet Malcolm was asked about writing her biography of the American poet Sylvia Plath, she compared her work on it with that of a professional burglar, "breaking into a house, rifling through certain drawers…and triumphantly bearing [the] loot away."[3]

Our friends, the dead, depend on us. Joseph Conrad wrote that those who are dead "can live only with the exact intensity and quality of the life imparted to them by the living."[4] It's up to us, then, the living, to keep them alive somehow in the stories we share. Unfortunately for the dead, it's not always the most supportive friend who gets to tell the story. As the famous Oscar Wilde quip attests, no matter how many disciples there may be, "it is always Judas who writes the biography."[5]

In one of his books about biography, Nigel Hamilton says "scratch any serious modern biography and love will be a predominant motif."[6] We all know that some love stories don't turn out well. Biographies, like memoirs, can be filled with acts of revenge. An editor friend of mine recently shared the opinion that when men write memoir or biography, they want to try to set the record straight, finally, and often by getting even. In contrast, the editor suggested that when women write memoir or biography, they tend to seek a new understanding of a particular relationship or experience. Literary biographer Hermione Lee says it doesn't matter whether the biographer is male or female; the most important point is what a biographer does *not* include. She sides with Julian Barnes when she says that biographies "are full of things that aren't there: absences, gaps, missing evidence, knowledge or information that has been passed from person to person, losing credibility or shifting shape along the way."[7]

I never met Henri. The Henri I have come to know is the prism-like person filtered though the memories of others, some of whom are indeed literal and figurative disciples of his. The disciples I met are the ones who, unlike Judas, did not slink away in the darkness. They stayed until the meal was over, and many attended the burial.

As a member of the growing international community of people who write about the life of Henri Nouwen, I like to think that I am neither Judas-like nor a burglar. I think of myself an observer at a distance who in the course of this project has discovered a friendship with someone who is dead. The Henri I befriended is the person I came to know as I listened to people who knew him well. In preparing a radio documentary about him for the Canadian Broadcasting Corporation with Michael W. Higgins, we heard friends and colleagues and former students as they painted their portraits with words. In these conversations with the living, twenty years after his death, Henri was a vital presence.

The more I listened, the more Henri shape-shifted, just as Hermione Lee suggested. In her analysis, biographical portraits are not fixed for very long. Mary Carruthers, in her fascinating books about memory in the pre-print medieval world, cautions us about the fragility of memories and the unreliability of documents. She advises us to interpret both carefully and to consider that what may be more truthful about them is not always their content: "That is *what* they remember, but rather their form and especially their ability to find out things, that is *how* they cue memories."[8] What was said and how it was said becomes the story. The transcripts of the interviews, like the medieval manuscripts that Carruthers describes, "do not resemble databases so much as they do maps for thinking and responding."[9]

Like every biography, what follows is a thinking and responding work in progress. A generation from now, as more letters and recollections surface, the contours of the mapped portrait of Henri will continue to evolve with more thinking and more responding. The book in your hands offers a composite portrait of Henri Nouwen, who was born January 24, 1932. This portrait is assembled from observations by a small but close group of people who knew him well, and from my own reading of his books. The conversations were mostly about the professionally engaged "Henris," and this is why I pay more attention in this biography to his experiences on this side of the Atlantic than his early years in the Netherlands. I try, though, to capture something of the spirit and intensity of his life, recognizing the impossibility of trying to capture in words the entirety of any person's life journey.

As people began telling their Henri stories, time and again, there would be a sudden rush of emotion and a necessary pause for a moment to recover as they struggled to continue. Their voices were altered, stirred by memories of someone no longer in their life yet still a vivid presence. They needed to recount their stories and impressions with accuracy and respect. The stories I listened to contained recurring images: Henri's sudden changes of mind, new challenges and old contradictions in collision, his clear strengths and the sometimes hidden weaknesses of this gifted individual, a creative artist who was also a wounded healer.

Listening takes effort and sometimes calls for subtle change of footwear as well as attitude, as Pope Francis explained recently.

> Listening means paying attention, wanting to understand, to value, to respect, and to ponder what the other person says. It involves a sort of martyrdom or self-sacrifice, as we try to imitate Moses before the burning bush: we have to remove our sandals when standing on the 'holy ground' of our encounter with the one who speaks to me. Knowing how to listen is an immense grace, it is a gift which we need to ask for and then make every effort to practice.[10]

As with any conversation, there were asides and diversions that explained certain situations. This book does the same thing with vignettes in each chapter. These detail certain events that had especially lasting consequences. I move through the sixty-four years of Henri's life as chronologically as possible, and in each chapter, I focus only on Henri's books from that particular time period.

I am thankful for the opportunity to discover a biographical friendship with Henri and the realization of the depth and continuing reach of his influence. This work is neither hagiography nor biographical hatchet job. I do not offer it as a *positio* by stealth for Henri's cause for beatification and canonization. I leave that for others. Like Henri's *Letters to Marc*, this work is written "as much for myself as for you," the reader.[11] Think of it as a letter that begins with "Did I ever tell you about this person who…?"

I use this image of a letter because of their importance for Henri. He received sixteen thousand of them, according to Gabrielle Earnshaw at the Nouwen Archive in Toronto. "Letter writing was something he took very seriously," she says. "He wrote about letter writing and the importance of letter writing as a form of ministry, as a form of friendship, as a form of retaining relationship, as a form of connection with community."[12]

Knowing that people he didn't know chose to write to him caught him by surprise. These letters had a direct effect on him, and he said they influenced not only his prayers but even his breathing and heartbeat.[13] He also wrote three enduring books in the form of letters: *Letters to Marc* (his nephew), *A Letter of Consolation*, written in 1982 to his grieving father, and *Life of the Beloved*, written in response to a challenge from a secular Jewish entrepreneur, writer, and friend. Fred Bratman asked Henri to write something useful about the spiritual life for him and his friends. He writes it as if he was addressing a dear friend he has come to know "as a fellow traveler searching for life, light, and truth."[14]

Henri was a fellow traveler in a rapidly changing Catholic culture. Richard Sipe, who first appears in this book as a Benedictine and fellow student with Henri at the Menninger Foundation early in their careers in psychology, will reappear later in a very different context. One night, as I took a break from writing, I went to the movies and was surprised when Richard Sipe suddenly made an appearance in the feature film *Spotlight,* which is about the *Boston Globe*'s coverage of the Boston archdiocese's sexual abuse scandal. The film is based on the work of the *Boston Globe*'s investigative team and the articles that resulted in their book, *Betrayal,* which also references the work of Richard Sipe. The team asserts that the problem in Boston was not unique, but "a microcosm of a festering sore on the body of the entire Church. If to some defenders it seemed like merely a brushfire, it was to others the greatest conflagration to face the Church in generations. It spread across the North American continent, stretched across to Europe, and scandalized Australia and parts of Latin America."[15] You don't see Richard Sipe onscreen; it's an actor, Richard Jenkins, who provides the voice of the California-based expert on celibacy and formation who takes part in teleconferences with the newspaper's team of journalists. In the midst of that clamor about credibility, leadership, and moral authority, I was reminded how Henri's spiritual authenticity stands apart as it also continues to engage people.

I think the actor who plays Sipe in that film would enjoy playing Henri. That voice! Dutch rolling and trilling and as smooth as Edam. There are some funny and really moving examples of Henri's voice in the Toronto archive. As I worked with them, I was fascinated by the sound. Dutch-speaking Henri spent most of his adult life living and writing in English, but if you listen to any recording of his voice from the 1970s and those from the 1990s, his accent never changes. Unlike many people who, like me, once they arrive on this side of the Atlantic, begin to drift toward a mid-Atlantic vocalization, Henri sounds decidedly and consistently Dutch. Henri's Dutch biographer, the late Jurjen Beumer, said it was the same whenever Henri spoke Dutch. "It's amazing! Some people go to the United States for maybe a year or two, and they love to have an American accent. Henri, when you hear him talking in the Dutch language, even after thirty years, you wouldn't say he had ever lived in the United States or Canada. He felt very connected with his own country, I think."

As I researched many biographies to see how they worked, I found one that, like this one, was written about someone twenty years after the person's death. It was Kevin Bazzana's biography of the Canadian pianist Glenn Gould, who incidentally was also born in 1932. Some key phrases grabbed my attention because of the way they also apply to Henri. Gould, like Nouwen, died young. His "untimely death at the age of fifty" shocked people and "stimulated new, widespread demand for his work." Bazzana then addresses the issue of legacy. "Since his death, the literature has grown exponentially...major biographies...books of photographs and reminiscences by people who knew [him], surveys of his work...more focused studies...conferences—scholarships, testimony, hagiography."[16] And especially this: "His posthumous reputation has been enhanced by the aura of the explorer, the rebel, the outsider that surrounds him." Bazzana's Gould "demonstrated even after death, a remarkable ability to capture people's imaginations, sometimes with the force of revelation."[17]

Isn't that Henri?

Before leaving Glenn Gould, he shares something else with Henri Nouwen in addition to 1932. By the time they were just six years old, each knew the career they would pursue. "As early as age five or six," Bazzana tells us, "Glenn had decided he would become a professional pianist."[18] Henri tells us, "Since I was six years old I have wanted to be a priest, a desire that never wavered except for the few moments when I was overly impressed by the uniform of a sea captain."[19]

As I read more biographies, I encountered several biographical techniques I wanted to avoid; for example, leading with a set of predetermined theories and forcing every aspect of a life to conform to them. Or identifying family traits as if dealing with the ingredients of some kind of genetically determined cake. I am not that kind of biographical baker. Instead, I looked to fiction for guidance. In the final section of *Middlemarch*, the novelist George Eliot gave me the approach that seemed to be the one to follow. She writes that it is the unfolding of a life story through time that captures our attention.

> Every limit is a beginning as well as an ending. Who can quit young lives after being long in company with them and not desire to know what befell them in their after-years? For the fragment of a life, however typical, is not the sample of an even web: promises may not be kept, and an ardent outset may be followed by declension; latent powers may find their long-awaited opportunity; a past error may urge a grand retrieval.[20]

I trace Henri's journey through its ardent outset in religious life and the emergence of his latent powers as a compelling speaker and writer. He stumbled several times before a long-awaited opportunity presented itself and which made the final decade of his life such a grand retrieval.

When he died in 1996, the generation that knew his works mourned him, and a new generation began to discover, in his absence, a thoughtful writer who managed to talk about difficult things concerning spirituality and faith, and ultimate meaning and death, in ways that are easily understood. With biography, though, even as new material surfaces, we still must start again from the beginning, as Kierkegaard (who will make cameo reappearances in chapters 2 and 7) cautions: "No generation begins at any other point than did the preceding generation, every generation begins all over again."[21] As that first generation mourned Henri in stories about him, they helped the next generation learn about him, and they also did what Michael Holroyd suggests people have done throughout history:

> By recreating the past we are calling on the same magic as our forbears did with stories of their ancestors round the fires under the night skies. The need to do this, to keep death in its place, lies deep in human nature, and the art of biography arises from that need. This is its justification.[22]

This, then, is an invitation to another generation of readers to begin a conversation with one of our friends, the dead. As you get to know him, you might find that he's a member of that sometimes ragged but always brave parade of inspiring individuals in the Christian tradition that we know as the communion of saints— even if they may not be fully signed members of that prestigious club. Yet.

CHAPTER ONE

CERTAINTY

❧ { 1932–1968 }

"I have come from somewhere and I am going someplace else."[1]

Like every year, 1932 was one of those years. In the midst of a bleak economic depression that continued to cast a confidence-crushing shadow across Europe and North America, some newborns arrived who, in time, would emerge from their distressed communities to leave their indelible stamp on the world. In the year that the seventy-seven-year-old John Philip Sousa died, the Italian novelist Umberto Eco; the mystical Russian filmmaker Andrei Tarkovsky, and his more urbane French filmmaking colleague, François Truffaut; the tortured American poet Sylvia Plath; and two nascent cardinals, Francis Arinze and Edward Egan, entered the world. A new member joined the Kennedy clan, Edward, or "Ted." Ready to take on Nashville, Patsy Cline and Johnny Cash. And months apart, Glenn Gould and Henri Nouwen—Henri in Nijkerk, the Netherlands, on January 24, and Glenn Gould in Toronto, on September 25.

After the sharp Dutch winter of 1932, the infant Henri Jozef Machiel Nouwen was readying to take his first steps for his proud and very Catholic parents, Maria (Ramselaar) and Laurent (senior) who married the previous year. The most frequently given descriptions of the Nouwen family present an emotionally nurturing and loving mother (one of eight siblings) who was creative, expressive, and deeply religious, and a somewhat distant and critical father (one of eleven siblings) who was a specialist in tax law and was successful and demanding. Together they raised four children:

Henri, then Paul (1934), then Laurent, (1944), and the next year, their daughter, Laurien. Henri's brother Laurent suggests that the typical portrayals of their father are oversimplified. "He was very intelligent, very industrial, a very factual man, and maybe he felt a little bit outside of this emotional relationship my mother had with Henri."

Events outside the close-knit Nouwen family circle threatened their entire future. Within a year of Henri's birth, Hitler was Germany's chancellor. By 1940, the Dutch people, according to their own queen, Wilhelmina, were "asleep on the pillow of neutrality."[2] Many German Jews had crossed the border for safety in the nonaligned Netherlands. Within hours of listening to Dirk Jan de Geer, their prime minister, assure everyone in a radio address that there would be no invasion, German bombs were falling on Rotterdam. Four days later, the city was in ruins, and the country surrendered.

Under the occupation, the same measures that had torn Germany asunder were imposed on the Netherlands. Food was rationed, and those not in the military could be forced to work for the Reich— anywhere. "No element of society remained untouched by the Nazis," write the sisters Kristen den Hartog and Tracy Kasaboski in their reconstruction of their family's experience of the occupation. Ominously, they add, that "for every act of rebellion, the Germans struck back, often aided by the Dutch who had sided with them."[3]

The Jewish community, some 140,000 at the time, was required to register to "ensure their safety, when in fact the record of who they were and where they could be found would facilitate their undoing."[4]

Cautious, the Nouwen parents moved with their children several times during the occupation, from Nijkerk to Venlo to Bossum to Scheveningen to The Hague, where Henri would eventually attend Aloysius College. Despite the uncertainty of life under occupation, the Nouwen family photographs from this era show a loving, affectionate, child-focused, multigenerational, and large circle of family and friends. The Nouwen children are invariably formally and elegantly dressed, even when out on their bikes. The privations of wartime occupation may have been kept away from the lens, but they had a major impact on the family's daily life. "The last years of the war were very difficult for the family: the famine," explains Laurent. "Henri and Paul had to go to the farms to find food and they went on those expeditions, which were adventures."

Looking back on this period of childhood forty years later, Henri also offers a hint about life under occupation. "I can still recall the infamous winter of hunger and the victorious entry of the Canadians in May, 1945. I've personally experienced the difference between 'being occupied' and 'being free,' so I know what a privileged individual I have been since 1945."[5] He keeps other details about his childhood very much to himself. "I am amazed how little I remember," he says, before presenting some fragments of memory: "Classmates laughing at me because I was cross-eyed, my first communion, the beginning of the war and my parents crying, the death of my grandmother and her funeral, Indian games and cowboy fights—but except for these flashes of memories, large empty periods."[6]

Walter was a rare remembered exception. When Henri was thirteen years old, his father gave him a goat to look after, named Walter. "I loved my little goat. I spent hours collecting acorns for him, taking him on long walks, and playfully fighting with him....

Walter and I were the best of friends."[7] One day, Henri found Walter's pen was empty. Someone had stolen the goat. There were serious food shortages in the waning days of the war. "I don't remember ever having cried so vehemently and so long.... My father and mother hardly knew how to console me. It was the first time that I learned about love and loss."[8]

Amid that otherwise large emptiness of childhood that he describes, there was one crystal clear moment of certainty. Henri said he knew by the time he was six his life's mission was to be a priest, and he played the role many times wearing child-sized vestments specially made for him. His mother's brother was a significant influence. "Uncle Toon" to Henri was Monsignor Anton Ramselaar, president of the minor seminary in Apeldoorn, where Henri would eventually begin formal studies for the priesthood. Later, Uncle Toon also played an important postwar role in Jewish-Christian relations in the Netherlands, "a bitter necessity considering the role of the churches during the holocaust," as Jurjen Beumer notes.[9]

When Henri was in grade school, Anne Frank and her family were hiding in their "Secret Annexe" on the upper floor of an office building at 263 Prinsengracht in Amsterdam, and Etty Hillesum was ninety miles away in the Westerbork transit camp. Each of them tried to understand their experience by writing about it. "The whole time I've been here I've longed unconsciously—and at times consciously—for trust, love and physical affection," wrote the fourteen-year-old Anne Frank two days before Henri's twelfth birthday, January 22, 1944. "This longing may change in intensity, but it's always there."[10]

Henri would eventually learn to live with that kind of unresolved longing too.

Months later, interned in Westerbork, from where she would soon be taken by train to Auschwitz and her death, the twenty-eight-year-old Etty Hillesum prayed, "God, grant me the great and mighty calm that pervades all nature. If it is your wish to let me suffer, then let it be one great, all-consuming suffering, not the thousand petty anxieties that can break a human being. Give me peace and confidence. Let every day be something more than a thousand everyday cares. All those worries about food, about clothing, about the cold, about our health—are they not so many denials of You, my God?"[11]

Henri would eventually be drawn to live and work with people broken by their limitations and their anxieties.

As he dreamed of the priesthood, surrounded by affection, and protected from much of the wartime horrors beyond the family homes and his classrooms, Henri still craved reassurance. "When I was a small child I kept asking my father and mother: 'Do you love me?' I asked the question so often and so persistently that it became a source of irritation to my parents."[12] His brother Laurent says this endured long after Henri's childhood. "Henri all through his life was questioning himself whether or not he was loved. He had great doubt."

This existential doubt is the source of Henri's genius, says the Jesuit spiritual director and former L'Arche chaplain Bill Clarke. Over their years working in different L'Arche settings, their paths would cross several times. Looking back, Clarke says that this nagging sense of doubt was, in fact, Henri's deep sense of woundedness and the result of not getting something that he sensed he needed from his parents. "Of course, none of us do," says Clarke, "though some of us get a little more than Henri did. He's not blaming his parents, it's just that for Henri, he was always in search of who he really was and where he really belonged. I think that search is where his wisdom, and where his gift, came from."

As the teenage Henri made it clear that the decision he made at the age of six was a genuine commitment, his father set some conditions. "'You are not ready to make a decision about the priesthood,' my father told me. 'You better wait until you are eighteen,'" writes Henri.[13] He dutifully obeyed. Then, on July 27, 1957, no longer a student at the seminary at Rijsenburg, he was welcomed into the priesthood by the Cardinal Archbishop of the Netherlands, Bernard Alfrink, who would play a significant role throughout Henri's priestly formation. Henri celebrated his first Mass using the golden chalice passed on to him as a gift by Uncle Toon.

What kind of 1950s priest would Henri become? Would he take on a large urban parish? Would he follow that typical academic and clerical sequence of advanced theological studies in order to teach seminarians and eventually advise his bishop and cardinal? Maybe a school chaplain?

In the pomp and circumstance of clerical life in the pre-Vatican II Catholic Church, Henri had a surprising yet calculated-sounding idea about the kind of priest he thought he could be. He made what was at the time a very courageous choice, given the deep suspicion of studies beyond the traditional bounds of classical theology. "I suppose that being the eldest son and part of a very ambitious family, I let the voice of upward mobility win out.... I became a hyphenated priest.... Priest-Psychologist. If somebody didn't like priests, they might at least like psychologists!"[14]

His Cardinal Archbishop may have had different plans for him, but, remarkably at that time in history, he supported Henri's pursuit of this nontraditional hyphenation, which required six more years of study at the relatively new Catholic University of Nijmegen, founded in 1923. A fellow student there who became his lifelong friend was Peter Naus. Peter first met the newly ordained Henri in 1957, and their professional and personal paths crossed many times until Henri's death.[15] "Henri majored in psychology from day one," Peter recalls.

> We studied phenomenological psychology. It means that rather than looking at human behavior from the outside—as is typical and was typical from the study of psychology in the time Henri and I were students—but look at it from the inside. From experience. Try to get into it, and try to describe it the best you can.

During these innovative studies for a priest, which began in the Netherlands and would continue in the United States, Henri was introduced to the work of Anton Boisen, a critical figure in the history of clinical pastoral education in the United States. Henri researched deep into this man's ideas and the practices that flowed from them. Boisen was another hyphenated professional. He was a clinical practitioner in a mental health institution and also a pastor. Henri eventually discovered how, despite Boisen's evident professional influence, he was a deeply damaged individual. Boisen had survived five major breakdowns in his adult life and spent significant time in a mental hospital—not as a chaplain or pastoral care worker, but as a patient. In Anton Boisen, Henri discovered an enduring archetype: someone dedicated to healing who was also struggling to resolve a great deal of internal messiness. This concept of the wounded healer became the subject for his dissertation.

Dr. Christopher De Bono is a medical ethicist and member of the Joint Centre for Bioethics at the University of Toronto and an expert on the work of Anton Boisen and its influence on Henri

Nouwen. He sets out the basic facts, outlining Boisen's autobiography: born in Indiana in 1876, Boisen studied forestry at Yale. In 1908, after just three years in that business, he felt called to ministry and enrolled at Union Seminary in New York. He was ordained a Presbyterian minister in 1912. Early in his ministry he had his first breakdown, which was treated as catatonic schizophrenia. In recovery, he struggled to make sense of his experiences and began to make both connections and distinctions between his religious experiences and his experiences of mental health crises. He realized that no matter which one you might choose to focus on, you can't address one without considering the other. From 1925 until 1954, when Boisen retired, he became a major figure in the development of clinical pastoral education in the United States. After retirement, he continued to write and give talks, until his mind began to wander. He died in 1965. In his 1960 autobiography *Out of the Depths*, Boisen wrote this about his mental crises,

> I have chosen deliberately to follow the thing out. I have been following a trail which has taken me through some very dangerous country. But I believe it has been worth while, and I would make the same choice again. Even this experience, painful though it is, may be an adventure of which use can be made.[16]

De Bono identifies Anton Boisen's influence on the young Henri Nouwen: "We see Henri Nouwen trying to understand the case method and its role in in the clinical pastoral education movement in the United States." Psychiatric care in the years following the Second World War

> was just beginning to move from custodial care to an idea that there may be something we can do beyond

custodial care, hence the introduction of other disciplines. This is one of Boisen's really important ideas. It is ground-breaking to start thinking about a person who presents as "mentally ill" and in fact what they may be doing is working out a crisis in their life. Boisen wanted to figure it out for himself because he went through this problem-solving experience. He went through this crisis and he didn't see that as a curse. He actually saw that as a blessing. So he is definitely a clinician. But he is also an educator. An understudied part of Anton Boisen is also that he was a pastor.

It was Boisen who promoted the concept of studying the person under your care as if they were a multifaceted living human document: "That's a phrase that has a lot of legs in the pastoral care movement," explains De Bono.

> What he meant was that we need to challenge not just science to take seriously the religious ideas that clients present us with, but we also need to challenge the Church to say that when we as ministers go into mental health centers, we don't "bring" theology to these people. What we actually discover in their lives is something of the revelation of God, something of the search for God.

Making such conceptual discoveries was not enough for Henri. He needed to see for himself. This became a recurring pattern throughout Henri's life and work. He sought out direct personal contact with such experts. His training in phenomenological psychology required him to get inside the story, to work face-to-face. De Bono describes the scene as Henri went off to meet this famous pioneer of the living human document concept and who had now become an actual living human document for Henri. It was August 1964, and Boisen had only a few more months to live. Henri was in the United States and decided to visit the Elgin State Hospital in Illinois to interview this famous curmudgeonly clinician, educator, and chaplain. He found "a very distraught, elderly man, frail, clearly suffering from passing delusions." Confused and alone, Anton Boisen died in a hospital bed in 1965.

De Bono draws out the connections between Henri's encounter with this "broken man at the end of his life" and Henri's insight as "he looks at that and he sees this woundedness that gives light." Henri would dig deeper into this image in the book he would eventually write. In *The Wounded Healer*, published in 1972, Henri begins to shift from the clinical to a more pastoral voice as he observes that "the wound of loneliness is like the Grand Canyon—a deep incision in the surface of our existence which has become an inexhaustible source of beauty and self-understanding."[17]

The Grand Canyon. Imagine what seeing, even contemplating that must have been like for Henri, who grew up in a country so flat that for centuries it was a damaged dyke away from being overwhelmed by the crashing waves of the North Sea. "I think there's a lot to mine there in terms of this man Henri Nouwen running out to meet Anton Boisen. He didn't just read about him. He actually went to meet him," adds De Bono.

As any researcher knows, start with one question and you are soon pushed and pulled and caught in an intricate web of new lines of investigation and never-ending connections. Henri's research into Boisen was like that. One of his links to understanding Boisen was the American psychologist Gordon Allport, who worked extensively in personality theory. It was Allport who directed Henri to the Menninger Foundation's program in religion and psychology in Topeka, Kansas. And it was there that Henri encountered Seward Hiltner, a specialist in pastoral counseling, and Paul Pruyser, whose research focused on psychology and spirituality. At this point in his life, it is almost as if Henri the priest-psychologist was on his way to becoming a psychologist-priest.

Enrolled at the Menninger Foundation in Topeka, Kansas, in 1964, Henri spent the next two years in a fellows program in spirituality and psychology. After this intensive program, he would return to the archdiocese of Utrecht. He now found himself in the vastness of America's heartland, bigger and wider than anything he had ever seen in the Netherlands. From the outside, the foundation's main building looked like any typical turreted nineteenth-century university or hospital institution with its imposing clock tower. The main difference, though, was that this campus spread out over acres of rolling grassy land, with trees and walking paths to the smaller buildings scattered through the grounds that housed the various psychiatry programs.

One of the fellows in the program was an American Benedictine, Richard Sipe, born the same year as Henri, who was studying the psychosexual dimensions of celibacy. "When we both were at Menninger's, I was the one concerned with spiritual development. He was the psychologist," Sipe explains. "As the years went on, that shifted because I spent all these years in clinical practice and he spent all these years in teaching, in which, as I followed his career, he became much less of a psychologist, and much more of the spiritual leader and spiritual guru. I think that was the development of his vocation."

Cardinal Alfrink came to visit Henri at the Menninger Foundation, perhaps to remind him that there was a Catholic community back in the Netherlands expecting to benefit from this new kind of research in psychology and spirituality. Before Henri returned home, and through an arrangement with Uncle Toon, who was working at the Second Vatican Council, he managed to spend several weeks at the Vatican to take advantage of the unique backstage view that his uncle was able to provide.

Henri was accumulating credibility, especially on the psychologist side of the hyphen, but where would he go with what he'd learned? Would he come home soon? His mother certainly wanted to know. She followed every detail of Henri's life in the letters they exchanged regularly. They are affectionate letters from a dutiful oldest son who loved to travel. He had already crossed the Atlantic several times as a volunteer chaplain on the transatlantic liners of the Holland-America Line. The first of those crossings had been especially poignant for him. "I can still see her waving from the quay of Rotterdam Harbor as the large ship *Statendam* slowly left its berth, taking me on my first trip to the United States," he later reflected.[18]

Henri was partway through his Menninger Foundation program when news reports started to cover the growing influence of Dr. Martin Luther King Jr. and the increasingly active civil rights movement in America. Henri felt compelled to be more than a bystander; he joined the march to Selma. His Benedictine colleague Richard Sipe remembers feeling challenged by this.

> The thing that was noticeable about Henri is his social activism, his social interest. He went down to the Selma march. So he brought a kind of interesting perspective on America and on American things that was more muted, I think, in the rest of us. We were interested but we didn't plunge in and we weren't active in the same way that Henri was. That was the distinct contribution

he made, that his energy was translated into activism, and his understanding of American life was very enlightening to all of us, and inspiring.

Of course, he wasn't the acclaimed Henri Nouwen at that point, so one doesn't see him in the photographs, linking arms with Rabbi Heschel and Dr. King. But Henri was there.

As his Menninger program came to a close, Henri had some important decisions to make. One of the research specialists at the foundation made him an offer that could keep him in the United States for an unspecified amount of time. John Dos Santos had been invited by the University of Notre Dame to set up a new psychology department. He thought that Henri, with his European training and his new North American insights, would be an interesting member of the faculty.[19] Initially hesitant because of his nontraditional credentials, Henri eventually agreed, and instead of returning to Utrecht, after consulting with his cardinal, he moved to northern Indiana.

In the competitive world of tenured academics, comparing credentials can consume a lot of energy. They influence salary, promotion, tenure, research grants, and the next position. Henri may have achieved the formal status of "Father" but he was not yet "Doctor" Nouwen according to American standards. Dos Santos offered him sessional or term contracts. Henri's energetic teaching style surfaced in the two years he was at Notre Dame, but it was not long before he realized that the university's research-driven, clinically focused program was not the kind of approach to psychology that really interested him. He had been chosen to join a team in a new university department only to discover that he really wanted to be chosen for something else, a more pastorally focused way of working, more akin to the clinical-pastoral approach that Boisen had pioneered. An anxiety, rooted in his childhood, also surfaced. "All my memories of being chosen are linked to memories of not being chosen," he would later write in *Life of the Beloved*.

> When I was not chosen for a soccer team, not chosen to be the leader of the Boy Scout patrol, or when I was chosen to be the "senior" of my ordination class or to be honored with special awards, there were always tears alongside smiles and smiles alongside tears. Competition and comparison always.[20]

In the spring of 1967, Henri, now priest-psychologist-professor, made his way from Indiana to the Abbey of Gethsemani in Kentucky. He decided it was time to meet one of America's most influential Catholics, Thomas Merton. This was the only time they would meet. It's clear he was in awe, and whenever he writes about Merton, Henri is at his most formal. He must have felt nervous as he walked down the grassy slope behind the chapel at Gethsemani and then over toward Merton's hermitage hidden in the distant trees. Merton's fellow monk and former student, John Eudes Bamberger—someone who would play a major role later as Henri's spiritual director—noted the importance of Henri's brief but important encounter with Merton. He says that Henri "got it" instantly.

> Henri Nouwen met Merton but once. Yet, by a sympathy of feeling and perception he has understood the central motivating force of Merton's life: meditation and prayer. He has seen this more truly and profoundly than some who, claiming to be intimate friends of Merton, have altogether missed the point of his work and life.[21]

Writing in his diary on the day they met, May 8, Merton interrupts his musing on the experience of being a stranger—"I know I do prefer solitude, and I want my solitude to be authentic"—to note his visitors. "Ran into Raymond's friend Alexis—the South African from Notre Dame—and Fr Nouwen (Dutch psychologist teaching at N D), had a good talk in the evening by the lake in Charlie O'Brien's pasture."[22]

Henri would eventually write a very perceptive book about Merton, first in Dutch and then reworked into English, but not just yet. Other issues intervened. During his now four-year sojourn in the United States, there were many convulsive world events. Activist Nelson Mandela was sentenced to life imprisonment in apartheid South Africa, Malcolm X was assassinated by coreligionists in New York City, American troops suffered terrible losses in Vietnam, and Che Guevara was killed in Bolivia. Assassin's bullets felled Robert Kennedy and Martin Luther King Jr.[23] Then, on December 8, 1968, at a conference in Bangkok, Thomas Merton, the monk he met in his hermitage that spring day in May was killed as he grasped a faulty electrical appliance. Like Boisen, Merton died alone—a haunting and recurring image for Henri.

As Christopher De Bono points out, Henri needed to meet the people he believed we could learn from. Merton was not the first. Meeting Boisen may have been troubling, but Henri realized the value of Boisen's work and, no less important, his courageous example. Merton had become an influential mentor for Henri long before he met him and continued in that role even after his death. In his 1972 English language version of the book about him, *Pray to Live*, Henri suggests that in the search for meaning in dramatic and breathtaking "Grand Canyons"—those big ideas or important people with reputations—we can overlook powerful examples that, in contrast, are quiet, small, and even mundane. When you can't find what you think you are looking for, you may be looking for the wrong things.

> It is perhaps always a bit disappointing when we look for an answer to the question of God in our lives. We are left only with titles of books, names of people and a few old facts. It seems all a bit lean and superficial. God doesn't let Himself get caught in titles, names and facts. But he lets Himself be suspected. And therefore it is only the one who prays to God, quite possibly the one who searches for silence himself, who can recognize Him in the many little ideas, meetings, and happenings on the way.[24]

Henri's extended North American interlude as a fellow and professor now over, he returned to his cardinal and his diocesan home in the Netherlands, where, as he suspected, a new kind of Catholic Church was taking shape.

CHAPTER TWO

THE FOCUS SHIFTS

⟨ 1968–1978 ⟩

"…at a great great great great price to himself…"

In 1968, Henri returned to the Netherlands with new insights that De Bono says challenged him

> to figure out what it is to be a professional minister. I mean, he was at the Menninger, he saw some of the best multidisciplinary, interdisciplinary connections, the perspective of religion in spirituality. He's beginning to struggle with this "psychologist priest" and "pastor." And his study isn't just his own life—that's going on in the pastoral care movement.

After thirty continuous years of education, Henri still needed more academic credentials. If he was going to gain credibility in the Netherlands or return to the United States to teach in a university, he needed that elusive doctorate. With his cardinal's seemingly ever-patient support, Henri set out to complete one at his alma mater, the Catholic University of Nijmegen. Anton Boisen, not surprisingly, was his focus. He began "writing up" his research using the case-study method and living human documents. In addition, he taught at the Pastoral Institute in Amsterdam, as well as in his home archdiocese in Utrecht at the Catholic Theological Institute, where he was hired as head of behavioral science.

Jurjen Beumer says that during the next few years of Henri's continuing studies, the hyphens Henri had begun to use, priest-psychologist-professor, needed further fine-tuning. What kind of priest? Exactly what kind of psychology? Teaching in which department? Beumer writes that "in these training courses the same tension existed between psychology and theology. Nouwen did not want to be strictly a psychologist. If he had to, then his preference was for pastoral psychology, but to do this he would have to become a theologian as well."[1]

The country he returned to was not the one he had left. Henri arrived in a Europe dealing with the consequences of major strikes and violent demonstrations, many of them student-led as events in one country were modeled in another. In 1968, *les évènements de Mai* brought universities and businesses in France to a standstill, riot police to the streets, and the government to the brink of collapse. Many participants ended up seriously hurt from physical confrontations with authorities. Demonstrators would dig up cobblestones to heave though the windows of businesses or at approaching police. One of their chants was *"Sous les pavés, la plage"* (Under the cobblestones, the beach). As they pulled up more and more stones, the newly revealed sand underneath made the street look like a beach.

Writing two decades later, Henri gives a hint of his frustrations as a postgraduate student struggling to complete a doctorate. "I vividly remember how one of my university teachers spoke for a whole year about anxiety in human life. He discussed in great detail the thoughts of Kierkegaard, Sartre, Heidegger, and Camus, and gave an impressive exposé of the anatomy of fear." Some of the students in the class asked if he would tackle the subject of joy before he concluded his course. "The next class he started hesitantly to speak about joy. His words sounded less convincing and penetrating than when he spoke about anxiety and fear."[2] After two more sessions, the professor gave up. He was, after all, reflecting the anxiety of that time in history when NPO, the public broadcaster in the Netherlands, daily carried stories about the student demonstrations in Europe, the war in Vietnam, and the fires and looting that had ignited parts of Detroit and Chicago in the aftermath of Dr. King's murder in Memphis. Momentarily putting the concept of joy to one side, Henri himself identified the "signs" of the late 1960s, as the era of "murder, hatred, anarchy, chaos, desperation, despair," and "a people full of anxiety."[3]

In the Netherlands, factions within the Catholic community were hurling metaphoric cobblestones at each other. As the documents of the Second Vatican Council were being digested, polarizing positions were being taken with splits in every direction. But rather than engage in Catholic factional politics in his homeland, Henri turned his attention to publishing his first book, and it was in English. *Intimacy: Essays in Pastoral Psychology* appeared in 1969 and was "born out of a two-year 'visit' to the University of Notre Dame," as he explains in the introduction. When you read these lines of the book, you see the influence of Boisen: "If there is a need for a new morality it is the morality which teaches us the fellowship of the weak as a human possibility."[4] And, "There is no human problem, human conflict, human happiness, or human joy, which cannot lead to a deeper understanding of God's work with man."[5]

Midway through, Henri introduces in print something that has become a slow-burning source of anguish and which, in time, will become a source of creative breakthrough for him. "Through Jesus," he writes, "we are invited to understand the homosexual existence as an expression of our basic human condition which is one of fear, anxiety, loneliness and, especially, homelessness, and is in essence a cry for the liberating power of faith, hope, and love."[6] That single sentence contains a set of key words that will resonate through the next phase of Henri's professional life: *basic human condition, fear, anxiety, loneliness, helplessness,* and *liberating power.*

"'There must be some way out of here,' Said the joker to the thief." That's from a song heard everywhere in Europe while Henri was contemplating his professional future. "All Along the Watchtower" is an opaque Bob Dylan song based on Isaiah 21: 8: "Then the watcher called out: Upon a watch-tower I stand, O Lord." In his version, guitarist Jimi Hendrix added additional layers to Dylan's folk idiom, a hazy psychedelic-sounding riff that takes on an ominous tone. Is it an approaching siren? The Hendrix version evokes a sense of uncertainty and imminent danger in an unsettled time. In the popular music world, when a musician takes on the work of another composer, this is called a cover, but if the original work is in the classical catalogue then it's called an interpretation. I use this musical image because what Henri does in *Pray to Live: Thomas Merton: Contemplative Critic* is put psychology and pastoral counseling to one side as he "covers" and "interprets" the work of Thomas Merton. *Pray to Live* focuses on the combination of prayer, contemplation, and social engagement that he identifies in Merton's life and books. It is a two-part creation, a mini-anthology or "cover" of Merton excerpts chosen by Henri, and the other is his interpretation of them. Henri uses the word "journalist" to capture Merton's skills of observation: "He is a journalist, a reporter, but a journalist who stops at everyday things and asks what their sense and meaning are."[7] From inside a cloister, "he in fact remained a journalist, a reporter who observes the world in which he lived, but under the critical eye of the gospel."[8] Merton is also a reporter of his own inner life who "put his daily feelings and thoughts under the critical eye of the gospel, and in the depth of solitude he found God, and his fellow human beings."[9]

There's also a line in which Henri is doing a bit of anticipatory autobiography. In describing what Merton *did* in his career, Henri identifies what he himself is *about to do* in the books, courses, talks, and retreats that will soon follow. "By his writing he had made himself and his most inner feelings and thoughts a public possession."[10]

Henri's Dutch public didn't consider him much of a "public possession" at the time, according to his brother, Laurent. He felt that Henri would soon be leaving the Netherlands once more.

> He found himself a stranger in this country. He was not well accepted. He was not understood. His call was not listened to. I think Henri's position was: first is my prayer, second are my friends I share my vocation with, and third, I go out in the world and try to bring the message. Now in Holland in those years, this was turned around. The priest was, first of all, socially involved, and if you have time left over, maybe you pray. That was not the sequence Henri was looking for. He was a man of prayer, first of all. His prayer was not rote prayer, it was creating silence for himself. Prayer was the essence of his life.

Just as Henri was now crossing the Atlantic with some frequency, so too was his reputation gaining momentum. His name began to appear in print on both sides of the Atlantic, and increasingly so on the American side. His article about attending Dr. King's funeral appeared in the *National Catholic Reporter* in 1968, and within a year of the release of his first book *Intimacy: Essays in Pastoral Psychology*, he published *Creative Ministry: Beyond Professionalism in Teaching, Preaching, and Counseling*. Both of these books grew out of his pastoral psychology experiences at the Menninger Foundation and, especially, the courses in ministry and psychology that he taught at Notre Dame. It's telling that Henri's first published book was written and published in English. Henri wrote all the books that followed in English, and he saw them published first in English. In his extensive publishing career, he wrote and published only three times in Dutch.[11]

It was on the strength of this growing international reputation as an influential teacher and articulate writer that Henri received an invitation to teach at Yale Divinity School. In 1971, once again he crossed the Atlantic, this time to join a Sister of Mercy, Margaret Farley, who recalled in an interview the immensity of this decision for Yale. "I was the first full-time woman on the faculty and Henri and I were the first full-time Catholics." Henri was hired as an associate professor of pastoral theology, but he added some conditions about the research and publishing he intended to do, as well as time away in the form of short sabbaticals between courses. Henri was what is known as a *doctorandus*, the Dutch term for a graduate who has successfully completed all the required course work and examinations, but not yet completed the dissertation.

Henri would have felt quite at home at Yale's Old Campus with its European feel, especially the long rows of elegant red brick buildings with gabled roofs and their geometrically balanced windows and courtyards with iron gates. They would remind him of *The Little Street*, a painting he would have seen in Amsterdam's Rijksmuseum, the work of one of Rembrandt's contemporaries, Johannes Vermeer. As he strode up Prospect Hill to get to the Divinity School, he would see in the distance the white column atop the chapel, and when he finally made it to the Quad, would see the how the buildings surrounding it give it the appearance of a large open-air cloister.

Henri's time as a faculty member of Yale's Divinity School was rich, dynamic, and creatively liberating. He brought the art of

Rembrandt into his lectures and taught a course entitled "The Compassion of Vincent Van Gogh."[12] He got his students to sing Taizé chant. He played "Epitaph" and other songs by the British "prog rock" band, King Crimson.[13] What his students observed was a physically awkward but highly energetic and enthusiastic teacher. When he looked out at them from the front of the class, which was often overflowing with students, he saw "a generation which has parents but no fathers, a generation in which everyone who claims authority—because he is older, more mature, more intelligent or more powerful—is suspect from the very beginning."[14]

The book that line is taken from, *The Wounded Healer*, set into motion the rise of Henri Nouwen as a major new and international Catholic voice. By 1974, credentials still in process, he was given tenure at Yale. As Margaret Farley says, "Yale is very tough with terms of giving tenure and there were no questions raised." Why was that? Because, she asserts, credentials notwithstanding, he was "a genius of spirituality."

Tension was growing despite his success, a tension he was not yet able to share with those around him. Externally, Henri's career both as a professor and author was taking off internationally. He was a young academic in a relatively new area of research that straddled psychology, spirituality, and pastoral counseling, and though his first language was Dutch, he wrote in highly accomplished, accessible, and idiomatic English. His work was being published not by small niche publishers but by major international publishing companies. Between 1969 and 1974, Henri published no fewer than seven books. Despite this external success, something was wrong. What he wrote in his journal about his difficulties and insecurities appeared only later, but he sought help from John Eudes Bamberger, the Trappist monk who studied under Thomas Merton, who was also now a trained psychiatrist.

After receiving tenure at Yale in 1974, Henri arranged for a formal seven-month sabbatical and moved to New York State to stay at the Abbey of the Genesee, where Fr. Bamberger would be his spiritual director. These two would strike any outsider as an odd couple: Henri over six feet tall, gangly, and constantly burning energy, and John Eudes Bamberger a good foot shorter, controlled, still, incisive, and precise. He "listened to me with care and interest," recalled Henri, "but also with a deep conviction and a clear vision; he gave me much time and attention but did not allow me to waste a minute."[15] Over the course of their frequent meetings, they concluded that the monastic life was not going to be the next step in Henri's life journey. Henri knew he would return to Yale and writing and teaching. His future would be marked by a different kind of discipline since, as he noted in his diary, "it was crucial for me to find concrete ways to prevent myself from drowning in activities and concerns on my return home."[16]

But Henri left the monastery with new a sense of integration.

> What is becoming clear is the need to enter into both realities—the priesthood as a function and a lifestyle and the spiritual life as a field of special concentration—more deeply, more fully, more extensively, and in a more scholarly way. 'Less speaking, more praying, more studying, and more writing' seems to summarize the best direction to take.[17]

That's what he would do. For a while.

Sabbatical over and now back teaching at Yale, Henri was soon on the book circuit with his 1975 publication *Reaching Out: Three Movements of the Spiritual Life*, as well as *The Wounded Healer*, in which, echoing Anton Boisen, he wrote, "The wound of our loneliness is indeed deep.... Making one's own wounds a source of healing...does not call for a sharing of superficial personal pains but for a constant willingness to see one's own pain and suffering as rising from the depth of the human condition which all men share."[18] (The penultimate word in that line is in conflict with the note Henri included in his introduction to the book about trying to respond to his friends who had already cautioned him about his use of male dominant language.)

In the foreword to *Reaching Out*, Henri says of himself what he had said earlier of Merton. "I wanted to write this book because it is my growing conviction that my life belongs to others just as much as it belongs to myself and that what is experienced as most unique often proves to be most solidly embedded in the common condition of being human."[19]

A tenured professor of pastoral theology at Yale, Henri knew the value of the sabbatical. Long or short, these are salaried opportunities for scholarly research and related travel. Between courses at Yale, Henri next arranged a five-month stay at the North American College in Rome. In the book he wrote while he was there, Henri demonstrates the historic subversive role of the clown. He goes one way with the title, *Clowning in Rome*, with its suggestions of hilarious antics on the Spanish Steps, and then he pulls the rug out from under your feet with the subtitle: *Reflections on Solitude, Celibacy, Prayer, and Contemplation.*

This book is a set of four lectures and a postscript, and it is Father Nouwen who is speaking to his vowed colleagues in religious life. He was following up on his Genesee resolution to make the spiritual life his focus. He stresses the importance of solitude, "the quiet place of listening."[20] Another lecture is intended for those in the helping professions. He warned of the dangers when they "quickly and quietly label people...giving us the illusion of understanding.

Not only psychiatric labels such as 'neurotic,' 'psychopathic,' or schizophrenic,' but also religious labels such as 'unbeliever,' 'pagan,' 'sinner,' progressive,' 'conservative.'" Such labels "provide a false understanding of the actual person and reveal more about our insecurities than about the real nature of our neighbors."[21]

In the chapter "Celibacy and the Holy" in *Clowning in Rome*, he writes that this way of life is "bound to touch those we encounter because it is a sort of ongoing street theater constantly raising questions in people's minds about the deeper meaning of their own existence."[22] This was written at a time when the number of people in religious life who were jumping ship was on the rise.[23] As priests opted to leave religious life in order to get married, for those who remained, it hurt.

Henri was aware of the research being done by his friend Richard Sipe about psychological and spiritual formation for the celibate priesthood and wondered

> if we have explored enough the very important relation-
> ship between marriage and celibacy. Lately I have become
> aware of this interrelatedness in a very painful way, real-
> izing the crisis of celibate people and the crisis of married
> people happened simultaneously. At the same time that
> many priests and religious persons began to move away
> from the celibate life, I saw many couples questioning the
> value of their commitment to each other.[24]

As he was working on the *Clowning* manuscript, Henri met with his old friend Peter Naus. "Henri told me in 1978 about his homo-sexuality. The context in which he told me was also such that I get a profound sense of his agony about that." He also turned once again to Sipe for advice. "He could not find what he called the mystical dimension of sexuality." Sipe describes this as Henri's "unsolved problem of his inner life. Not that he wasn't integrated. He was an honest guy, and he was certainly a celibate practising person, at a great great great great price to himself. But his sexual orientation was that unfinished piece of business that he took to the grave with him."

Henri, now forty-six, faced a familiar crisis in the life of most adult children. Earlier in 1978, his parents flew to the United States for a short visit with him, during which his mother became unwell. When his parents returned to the Netherlands, the seriousness of her condition was identified. It was a cancer that required urgent surgery. Henri knew he had to be with her in the hospital in Nijkerk. He remembered other journeys to the family home. "Whenever I came home, whether I was eighteen or forty years old, my mother would stay awake worrying about her child until she was sure that he was safely in bed!"[25] This time it would be different. He sat in the plane, numb. "Above the cold North Atlantic, I felt alone. Not lonely, not depressed, not anxious, not afraid, but alone in a new way. My mother was dying. She was waiting for me to come, she wanted to see me and to pray with me."[26] He arrived in time. "I kissed her forehead and touched her hand. Words were hardly possible or necessary."[27] On Monday, October 9, 1978, she died in the hospital room as Henri was outside in the corridor, busy with a telephone call. Her passing "was hardly noticeable," explained his father. Henri was scorched with the realization: "I was not at her bedside." Then another shock. "It slowly dawned on me that she who had followed every decision I made, had discussed every trip I took, had read every article and book I wrote, and had considered my life as important as hers, was no longer."[28]

Henri turned his attention to his father. After her death, Laurent noted, "My father started to correspond with Henri, quite a substantial correspondence, but it never got to the same intimacy as with my mother. I think my father would be more like an advisor."

In the midst of this grief, Henri chose to remember his mother in an almost sacramental way. "It means making her a participant in God's ongoing work of redemption by allowing her to dispel in me a little more of the darkness and lead me a little closer to the light."[29]

That light was still flickering, but it was on the other side of the Atlantic. Henri was once more on his way back to North America. Returning to Yale was something he did not want to consider. Somehow, the university no longer felt like home. Still, he was long past the point in his life when the Netherlands was the place he could remain. Where his next home might be in the vastness of the United States was a piece of unsettled business in need of some attention.

After the flight from Schiphol to New York, Henri made his way, not to New Haven and Yale, but toward Rochester and then over toward Piffard and the Abbey of the Genesee. There, in the austere chapel with its walls of large round stones, he would contemplate the possibility of dropping at least one hyphen (professor) and possibly adding another to his list of priest-psychologist-author. This new role might, after some more reflection, be "missionary."

In his diary, Henri wrote, "I left the Divinity School...and started to prepare myself for a more systematic discernment of a possible vocation in Latin America."[30]

CHAPTER THREE

WHAT KIND OF PEACE IS THIS?

{ 1978–1985 }

"I never realized that broken glass could shine so brightly."

It was the Church triumphant. "As the Legate approached in the deepening dusk, devout Catholics knelt in adoration of the Eucharistic Presence," reported *The Tablet* in 1910. "The odour of incense was heavy in the air. The crowds were tired, but their piety seemed indefatigable. Previous to the Legate's approach there had been numerous salutes fired from the mountain and the peal of bells in the temporary belfry mingled with the roar of bursting shells."[1]

The event was the 1910 Eucharistic Congress in Montreal and crowd control was a concern.

> So great was the packed mass of people about the Cathedral that more police had to be summoned to assist in keeping the children from being crushed. Several women fainted in the crowd, and had to be taken out by the police. From the Cathedral steps nothing could be seen but a sea of heads. A pretty scene was enacted when twenty boys, aged about ten years, dressed as knights of old, carried a magnificent floral basket to present to his Eminence, who smilingly acknowledged it as they stopped before him to receive the blessing.

Among the thousands attending this event presided by his eminence Cardinal Vanutelli, the papal representative sent to Canada by Pope

Pius X, were two American priests, James Anthony Walsh from Massachusetts, and Thomas Frederick Price from North Carolina. Each was deeply committed to Catholic missionary work. It was at this congress in Montreal that they formulated plans for a new kind of seminary and training center in the United States for Catholic missionaries. Within a year, they received papal approval for their Catholic Foreign Mission Society of America, known by its more familiar name today, the Maryknoll Fathers and Brothers, founded in 1911, and the Maryknoll Sisters, founded the following year. It was Maryknoll missionaries in Bolivia and Peru who hosted and supported Henri in his tentative immersion in missionary solidarity work outside of Europe and North America.[2]

Earlier in 1975, in *Reaching Out,* Henri had written, "When God has become our shepherd, our refuge, our fortress, then we can reach out to him in the midst of a broken world and feel at home while still on the way."[3] Now this less-than-practical, European-trained priest was well on the way to witnessing unrelenting poverty, human rights violations, and unpredictable violence.

First, he turned to language training at the Maryknoll language school in Cochabamba, Bolivia. As a pastor, teacher, and especially as a writer, Henri appreciated the power of words. He also knew their weakness when they may be linguistically correct but remain disconnected from the culture and experience of the people he wanted to communicate with. "I am learning that I am living in another world, and that words that can renew minds and hearts at one time and place might have a dulling and even deadening effect at another time and place," he reflected.[4]

While Henri was in Bolivia and Peru—and then, a few years later, in Guatemala—audiences in North America were learning about the precarious conditions in these countries simply by switching on a radio or television. With the development of new satellite uplinks, journalists in the 1970s and 1980s were able to file stories from inside the action. Their reports changed the way we experienced news. Radio newscasts from the world's hot-spots featured the thrumming of helicopter blades, sudden bursts of machine-gun fire, people yelling as they ran for cover. Journalists worked hard to keep the human or social justice component of these events from getting lost under the noise and spectacle of all the military and paramilitary action. Their reports taught many of us some new words and phrases: *junta, drug cartel, death squad, guerilla.*[5]

Country by country, reporters told us about military governments and disenfranchised indigenous peoples. We learned about National Guard units that were really guns for hire, mass killings, and the FMLN, El Salvador's Farabundo Marti National Liberation Front. From Peru, we were introduced to seemingly gentler phrases, such as *Sendero Luminosa* or "Shining Path," words that actually meant horrific violence. We also learned another acronym, MRTA: *Movimiento Revolucionario Túpac Amaru.* From El Salvador, we also heard than on March 24, 1980, Archbishop—now Blessed—Oscar Romero had been killed by a single bullet as he said mass in the chapel of the Divine Providence Hospital in San Salvador.

Bolivia, during the time that Henri was there, was ruled by a military and unstable government that faced an endless series of coups and counter coups. Its survival depended on a lot of drug money and even more ammunition.

Peru, during the time that Henri was there, had recently shifted from a military to a civilian government. The former president, Fernando Belaúnde Terry, ousted in a military coup twelve years earlier, was returned to power democratically in 1980. Military or civilian, the government still had to deal with powerful drug lords and unresolved internal conflicts throughout the country.

First impressions can be dangerous. Shortly after he arrived in Peru, Henri witnessed a large religious procession. "As soon as the bystanders realized that I was a priest, they let go of their inhibitions, handed me their children to lift above the crowds, and told me about their joys and sorrows."[6] It was not long before he encountered another reality altogether when his Maryknoll hosts told him about "the truth of the mass murders that destroy the lives of thousands of civilians, men, women, and children; of the indiscriminate killings to terrorize the poor; and of the selective and well-planned elimination of the leaders of the opposition, whether they are church leaders or political leaders."[7]

Henri found himself in a bewildering and contradictory setting. "With a proper burial, a death, even a murder, can be mourned and life can go on. But the uncertainly of a disappeared person's fate adds a new dimension to human suffering."[8] As much as he tried to imagine himself living in these precarious conditions, month by month, he eventually conceded that this was probably not the time for any such radical action on his part. "I have learned that this is not the time for speaking but for listening; not a time for initiatives but for waiting; not a time to offer leadership but a time to let go of old and cherished ideas and to become poor in spirit. Since we can learn from our mistakes, I might as well use this experience as a way to recall that these are times to be silent."[9]

This sounds like someone on a retreat, except that this one is not taking place in a bucolic rural retreat center with nicely manicured grounds and an elegant chapel with stained-glass windows. His published journal, *¡Gracias!*, presents a different Henri in a different voice, as in the dusty heat and humidity, he looks at the shanty dwellings, poor people struggling every day, and hungry children everywhere. This time his writing seems tentative and confessional. Then, almost as an aside, he outs himself as someone dealing with depression. "Every time I slip into another depression I notice that I have given up the struggle to find God and have fallen back into an attitude of spiteful waiting."[10]

Previously, at the Abbey of the Genesee, it was to John Eudes Bamberger that he turned to for guidance and support. There, in Peru, he met with a Dominican priest and theologian, Gustavo Gutiérrez—affectionately known as the father of liberation theology. Henri sought out this diminutive figure with a powerful international influence. Henri would recognize the energy of a focused and powerful performer in the way Gutiérrez spoke. His message was challenging but delivered with a warm, encouraging, and often shy-seeming smile. Gutiérrez makes people protective of him because (there's no other way to describe it) he has the apparent vulnerability of a child, despite his obviously adult body. Standing close, Henri would tower over this small man who was only four years older than he. As he watched Gutiérrez at work, Henri saw "a genuine theologian, a man who breaks the bread of God's word for thousands of people and offers hope, courage, and confidence." And he also noticed something else. "What struck me most was Gustavo's ability to integrate a spirituality of struggle for freedom with a spirituality of personal growth."[11] Henri certainly knew about the difficult challenges of integration and personal growth.

Curiously, Henri also turned to composer Leonard Bernstein to help him explain the struggle of keeping action and reflection at the heart of ministry and mission, while holding it all in some kind of balance. Writing in the high humidity of Peru, Henri remembered a performance in Washington a decade earlier. Bernstein's

Mass: A Theatre Piece for Singers, Players, and Dancers was commissioned to open the John F. Kennedy Center for the Performing Arts in Washington, DC, in 1971. It follows the structure of a Catholic Mass with Hebrew texts and additional words written by Stephen Schwartz, famed for the musical *Godspell*. *Mass* is part liturgy, part dance, part rock and roll, and part oratorio. Bernstein blends many musical styles in this work for a chorus of dancers and singers, children, soloists, and full orchestra. The central character is the Celebrant who experiences a dramatic crisis of faith. In the final section of the piece, he is overwhelmed by a cacophony of demands from his congregation. "What do I believe, and how do I answer all these questions that this congregation and these people from the world have asked me?" he sings in anguish. Members of the congregation lift him above their heads, then, in an angry outburst, he "hurls the raised sacraments to the floor."[12] As the shards lie shattered on the ground, the Celebrant suddenly notices how, when broken, the glass shines even brighter.

Mass ends with the Celebrant encircled by a chorus of children, dancers, and singers. Bernstein describes the stage action he wanted:

> Two slow chains of embraces begin, one originating with the boy, the other with the man.... As the canon continues, they are gradually joined by other couples, eventually by the entire cast. The chains of embraces continue, culminating in a joining of all hands.... The Boys' Choir...fill the aisles, bringing the touch of peace to the audience, saying with each touch, "Pass it on."[13]

Henri wrote twice about this climactic moment in *Mass*. The first time, in his Latin American journal, is brief: "This, to me, is what ministry and mission are all about. Ministry is entering with our human brokenness into communion with others and speaking a word of hope."[14] The second time, written a decade later (which means he was then recalling a performance twenty years after seeing it), he adds even more detail.

> As he walks slowly through the debris of his former glory—barefoot, wearing only blue jeans and a T-shirt—children's voices are heard singing, "Laude, laude, laude"—"Praise, praise, praise." Suddenly the priest notices the broken chalice. He looks at it for a long time and then, haltingly, he says, "I never realized that broken glass could shine so brightly." Those words…capture the mystery of my life.[15]

Leonard Bernstein struggled to complete *Mass* in time for the opening because, as his biographer, Humphrey Burton writes, his goal "was to create something that was, to use his own phrase about Beethoven, accessible without being ordinary."[16] For the Celebrant, Bernstein envisioned "not only St. Francis" says Burton, "but also the incarnation of Bernstein himself—the child inside the man who, like his image of Beethoven, 'never grew up, and to the end of his life remained a creature of grace and innocence and trust.'"[17]

Henri's recollections of that single moment in *Mass* are separated by what will be his most personally challenging yet most creative decade. He saw himself mirrored—personally, professionally, and so accurately—by Bernstein's Celebrant. Henri was not alone in this. In a letter to Bernstein, the late Right Reverend Paul Moore Jr., the former Episcopalian bishop of New York, wrote:

> In many ways it's the story of my life. I could deeply identify with the inordinate demands people make upon the church and the priest and with the deep revulsion

one sometimes feels toward the role. Using the priest's collapse, if you will, as a symbol of the sacrifice of the Mass which in a sense brought about the possibility of the resurrection scene in the end was a brilliant stroke on your part.[18]

Unlike Bernstein's Celebrant, however, Henri didn't collapse in a heap on the floor as a consequence of these difficult and dangerous months in Bolivia and Peru. He did admit feelings of "loneliness, isolation, and separation," though.[19] He also hit a dangerous midlife moment in the celebration of his fiftieth birthday. "I hope that by concluding here half a century of living, I am perhaps moving toward a new way of living and working in the future."[20]

Perhaps.

There was another deeply somber event to remember. December 1981 was the first anniversary of the rape and murder in El Salvador of Jean Donovan, a lay missionary; Maryknoll sisters Ita Ford and Maura Clark; and Dorothy Kazel, an Ursuline sister. On December 2, 1980, Jean Donovan and Dorothy Kazel were at the San Salvador airport waiting for the arrival of Ita Ford and Maura Clarke, who were returning from a Maryknoll meeting in Nicaragua. Their flight arrived, but the four never returned from the airport. Their colleague and Maryknoll Sister Madeline Dorsey was alarmed as the entire mission team lived under constant threats because of their solidarity work with the marginalized, especially the indigenous communities. A cautious search was organized.

> The search went on until noon on Dec. 4, when a farmer told his pastor that he had been forced to bury "four unidentified white women." We "flew" in Paul's jeep to the very concealed area where they were reported buried. [Paul is Father Paul Schindler, head of the mission team.]

Then came the painful extraction of the four—piled one on top of the other. Jean was first, her lovely face destroyed. Dorothy had a tranquil look. Maura's face was serene but seemed to utter a silent cry, and last little Ita. I went forward to wipe the dirt from her cheek and place her arm at her side. We Sisters fell to our knees in reverence.[21]

After the emotion-filled ceremony to remember these four martyred women just one year after their murders, Henri noted in his diary, "It was a moving service in which faith and hope dominated the sadness."[22]

Henri's book *¡Gracias!* is about culture shock: the discomfort that surfaces after you leave the smart arrival hall and are driven through sights, sounds, smells, and scenes that you have seen in documentaries and are now experiencing firsthand. Much of Henri's discomfort and restlessness in Latin America was already in his suitcase when he arrived. He was personally invested in and did connect to the families and the communities he lived in, and he writes respectfully and sensitively about their lives and "the stories about deportation, torture, and murder we hear every day."[23] Yet, at the same time, these courageous families seem to serve as living human documents in his ongoing research on a case study of himself. He's having trouble straddling yet another hyphen. Henri the observer has taken over from Henri the participant, Henri the writer from Henri the missionary, and in this, he joins that long line of writers who have struggled to balance both sides of a professional hyphen. The famous American poet and medical doctor, William Carlos Williams, had to keep reminding himself to see his patients as people in need of his medical care and not only as potential images and metaphors for his poetry. He once wrote "I learn so much on my rounds, or making home visits. At times, I felt like a thief because I heard words, lines, saw people and places—and used it in my writing…. There was something deeper going on, though—the *force* of all those encounters. I was put off guard again and again and result was—well, a descent into myself."[24]

Henri was certainly familiar with that sense of a descent into himself. Perhaps, when he looked closely at the mission team and the families they worked with, he could see the possibility of another way of life in a community, one he had yet to experience for himself. He was able to sketch out its characteristics, though.

> The core of this idea is that of living among the people to learn from them…all that we see and hear can become a rich source for locating the presence of God among his people. It would become *a ministry of presence…a mutual ministry of receiving and giving.* It would be contemplation in action, celebration and liberation, study and work, ascetic and festive, fraternal and hospitable.[25]

Here, Henri was describing a kind of community that already existed. It's the one that Jean Vanier was striving to build in the communities of L'Arche. In 1964, Jean Vanier, son of Canada's Governor General,[26] was in France and seeking guidance from his spiritual director, Pere Thomas, a Dominican. Vanier was horrified by the treatment of people with developmental disabilities in French institutions. He imagined a different noninstitutional approach. Rather than become theoretical about it, he took matters into his own hands. Vanier invited two young men with disabilities and who had been institutionalised, Raphaël Simi and Philippe Seux, to live with him instead in a small cottage in the village of Trosly-Breuil, about an hour north of Paris. Raphaël

Simi had contracted polio and had a neurological condition which caused him to lose his speech and become hemiplegic. When he was two years old, Philippe Seux had contracted encephalitis, delaying the development of his intellectual abilities.[27]

Vanier's idea was that they would live simply as a family, not as if they were in a smaller version of an institution. Vanier was not their caregiver and they were not his charges. Together they would discover *how* to live together, learning with and from each other. He named the place "L'Arche" after Noah's ark. ("When the bow is in the clouds, I will see it and remember the everlasting covenant between God and every living creature of all flesh that is on the earth" [Genesis 9:16].) Slowly, this example of a small home-based community that brings people with and without disabilities together became a model to be emulated, turning a long tradition of institutional care for people labeled "the disabled" upside down. Raphaël Simi and Philippe Seux are now considered the cofounders of L'Arche with Jean Vanier.

All of this was still a nascent idea for Henri. He would, in time, discover for himself and in a very authentic way the countercultural approach of L'Arche. In Jean Vanier's words, "We are people with and without intellectual disabilities living mutually transforming relationships in communities that become signs of peace in the world."[28] Before Henri would encounter this way of life he would have a few anguish-filled years ahead of him.

As his brief time as a hyphenated missionary in South America came to an end, Henri wondered if "going north still means going home."[29] Home for the time being would be in the mercy-filled embrace of St. Bernard of Clairvaux at the Abbey of the Genesee, and the pursuit of even more knowledge concerning what kind of life he would pursue next. In a sermon, St. Bernard advises that "your self-knowledge will be a step to the knowledge of God; he will become visible to you according as his image is being renewed within you."[30]

Robert Ellsberg takes up the story of Henri's return to the United States that began with an invitation to join Henri at a special gathering at the abbey in Piffard, New York, timed to celebrate Henri's twenty-fifth anniversary as a priest. "He had been in Latin America for a year, but he'd come back to Genesee and he'd invited hundreds of people to come and celebrate. But beforehand, he invited ten or so friends to come and spend a week with him in prayer and reflection, a kind of retreat." Robert Ellsberg was in that select group and was looking forward to meeting the Genesee community of Trappist monks. "I had been very affected by Thomas Merton and Trappist spirituality. It was very attractive to me, I was a recent convert, uncertain of my own vocation and where I was heading. It was a really wonderful few days," he recalls.

> I remember his making a speech in which he thanked the Abbot of Genesee for offering this kind of home to him. He said, "I've been wandering for many years, and finally, here at Genesee, I feel I've found my true home." About a week later when I was back, he called and said, "I've been offered a job at Harvard Divinity School and I think maybe I should take this job. What do you think?" I said, "Well, I thought that Genesee was going to be your true home now," and he said, "Well, the abbot says maybe it's not such a good idea for me to do that."

In 1983, Henri set off for Cambridge, Massachusetts, the classical red-brick austerity of Divinity Hall, and the grey-stone gothic facade of Andover Hall at Harvard.

Robert Ellsberg and Henri Nouwen would, in time, establish an effective editor/publisher and writer relationship, one that resulted in two of Henri's enduring works, *With Burning Hearts* and *Adam: God's Beloved.* These books—the second published posthumously and very widely translated—added to Henri's international reputation as one of the foremost pastoral voices on contemporary Christian spirituality. Such writer/editor relationships endure ups and downs and frequently become deeply personal. When Robert was invited to work as editor-in-chief at Orbis Books, the publishing company established by Maryknoll, he remembered asking Henri for his reaction.

> "Well, if somebody were to ask me about your fit here, I would say intellectually it's an excellent match. Perfect person for the job. But I don't know if you really have the human gifts for that kind of work, being able to work with people." And I was kind of astonished, and thinking what on earth is he talking about?

The penny dropped. In 1976, Robert had been the editor of *The Catholic Worker*—the penny-a-copy newspaper founded by Dorothy Day in 1933. As a young enthusiastic editor, Robert had asked the Yale professor with the reputation if he had anything that the newspaper might publish. Henri sent three pieces for him to look at, and Robert says, "I have to say, I wasn't terribly impressed. They seemed abstract to me, kind of idealistic and a little pious. And I said, 'Do you have anything else maybe that we could look at?'" Henri's reaction came as no surprise.

> He was understandably miffed and said, "Well, I've just given you three articles." I realized then that I had not handled this very well, and said, "Well, of course we want

to publish one of these excellent articles." Which we did. But he never offered anything else, and I never asked. That was our first encounter. I wouldn't have thought from that that we would have gone on to have a long and significant and professional friendship as well, when I became his editor at Orbis Books.[31]

Author, musician, and retreat leader Robert A. Jonas knows a great deal about Henri's time at Harvard Divinity School. "Jonas"— as Henri insisted on calling him—is the founder and director of a contemplative sanctuary for Buddhist-Christian dialogue in Northampton, Massachusetts, called the Empty Bell. After attending some of Henri's talks, Jonas was interested enough to want to get to know more about him and perhaps even invite him to be his spiritual director. As they began to discuss this, their roles started to reverse.

> Our conversation kind of tacked, like a sailboat tacks in the wind, back and forth from psychology to spirituality and back and forth. It was a lot of fun. As we talked, I began to feel that he had, we both had, some things to work out, let's put it that way. He was very interested in what I had to say about growing up with certain kinds of parents, like his and we at one point decided that—I don't know how this happened, I can't remember the exact details—but that I knew more about benefitting from therapy than he knew, and he wanted some help with some of his growing up issues. So we sort of framed it, the tables became turned briefly, where instead of him being my spiritual director I was his therapist in a way.

After a few months, they abandoned this confusing dynamic. Fortunately for them, a deep friendship survived. "He felt sort of ostracized by the professors at Harvard, that he wasn't a serious enough theologian, that his emphasis was so pastoral as to be not unintellectual, but coming from the heart rather than the head," says Jonas.

Theirs was an intense relationship. "Henri was gay. I knew that from the beginning of our relationship, and although I'm heterosexual there was never anything sexual between us," explains Jonas, "but we were very close." Henri talked about his struggles with sexuality and Jonas suggested that he perhaps might consider coming out as a priest "to lead a movement within the Roman Catholic Church that would help a more gay-friendly communion. But that wasn't going to happen."

Henri did become part of the Jonas family, living with them for months at a time. He was there when their son Samuel was born, and three years later, in 1992, he helped Jonas and his wife Margaret when their second child, Rebecca, died within three hours of being born. "He said, 'Jonas, you know that Jesus lost Rebecca too.'"[32]

As he had at Yale, Henri brought the artwork of Rembrandt and Vincent van Gogh into his courses at Harvard. "Look at Rembrandt and van Gogh. They trusted their vocations and did not allow anyone to lead them astray."[33] "Their lives and their art heal and console me more than anything else."[34] Henri was familiar with the van Gogh letters in which Vincent articulates his faith, his sense of mission, and also great outrage concerning his father. There's a detail in these letters that serves as a poignant counterpoint to a number of issues during Henri's increasingly difficult time at Harvard. In 1880 Vincent was twenty-seven, and his father, convinced that his son was deranged, tried to place him in the "lunatic asylum" in Geel, in Belgium. Vincent resisted and wrote about this event several times in letters to his brother, Theo. "My personal liberty may not be infringed. I told my Father that plainly enough at the time of the Geel affair when he wanted to pack me off to a madhouse."[35] "I tell you, if he dares to attempt something like that, I will stand up to him to the utmost."[36] "I would like Pa to have a fresh and clear impression of a new future for me, to see me here in surroundings very different from what he may imagine, for him to be completely reassured about my feelings towards him, for him to have confidence in my future and put wardship or Geel a thousand miles from his thoughts."[37]

What is this place, Geel, that triggered such a strong response? A report written by a visiting medical doctor just a few years before Vincent almost ended up there makes it clear. Dr. Mundy noted in his 1861 report for a British medical journal that the Belgian Government sent only the most incurable cases to the asylum at Geel.[38] He then goes on to explain Geel's unique and curious role in the history of psychiatric and mental health care that dates back to the seventh century:

> Among those who settled in this little colony were the daughter of an Irish prince and a missionary named Gerrebert who had converted her to Christianity. The cause of their flight from her father's house appears to have been his anger at the virtuous and Christian conduct of the Princess Dymphna. Their behaviour while at Geel secured for them the affection and respect of the other residents. This happiness did not last long, for the irritated father pursued them to their retreat, and ordered the death of his daughter and the priest. The latter was immediately slain, but none being found among his retinue who would execute his unnatural vengeance on

the youthful Dymphna, he slew her with his own hand. Among the spectators of this cruel martyrdom were some persons labouring under insanity, and such is said to have been the effect of the scene that their deranged faculties were roused into healthy action, and the former lunatics became sane in mind. In a barbarous and superstitious age, it was natural that an occurrence like this should be associated with a belief in its miraculous character, and, accordingly, to the virtues of the pious girl were imputed the remedial power. Henceforth Saint Dymphna was looked upon as the patron saint of the insane, and numbers of those mentally afflicted were brought to her tomb in hopes of some miraculous cure.[39]

In the Middle Ages, St. Dymphna's shrine in Geel became increasingly hospital-like as hundreds of pilgrims sought cures there. It would be of little consequence to such pilgrims to learn that historians consider Dymphna's life "almost wholly fictional."[40] David Farmer concedes that although her story may be "folklore," Geel itself does have an important place in the history of compassionate care for those who are mentally ill. In Geel, local families opened their homes to troubled souls who traveled, or were sent there, in the hope of a miracle.[41] By the time Geel surfaced as a possible solution for the van Gogh family, ideas about psychiatry and mental health had shifted from hoping for miracles to identifying clinically approved approaches, typically in those days straps and restraints. All the while, Geel combined the timeless hospitality of its religious origins with the clinical practices of the late nineteenth century. In addition to the asylum, another kind of care was provided by *nourriciers*—caregivers in the community who were paid for their hospitality services for their incurable guests they welcomed into their homes. Geel became the subject of much research into the interplay of clinical or institutional support and humanitarian family support.

Geel, metaphorically speaking, is not very far from the world of Jean Vanier and L'Arche. Of course, L'Arche works with individuals living with very different issues: intellectual and developmental disabilities rather than psychiatric disorders. Nevertheless, the *foyers* (or hearths) of L'Arche are an enlightened form of Geel's *nourriciers.* That word has associations of nurse, nanny, foster care, and nourishment which are incompatible with the very different principles of L'Arche, where people with disabilities are not thought of as children in need of watchful parents. Jean Vanier has always avoided using language that suggests any condescending kind of care. But Geel and L'Arche both illustrate a fundamental principle that noninstitutional care and non-exclusionary community building are basic to the ecology of human compassion and development.

The fragile Vincent van Gogh, suspicious of his father's actions, became an enduring symbol for Henri. In her book about van Gogh's spirituality, Carol Berry writes that Vincent "was a man who sought with all his being to reveal his love for the Creator and for all Creation. Henri Nouwen called Vincent his 'saint' and invited his students to join him in studying the art and life of this artist who had touched him so deeply."[42] Although completing his own book on Vincent's spiritual vision proved to be difficult because other matters of unsettled business demanded his attention, you can sense Henri's approach in Carol Berry's book, especially as she had access to Henri's notes as she wrote it.

Unable to complete his book about van Gogh, Henri did something familiar when he sensed he was in trouble. He turned to a trusted old friend. A decade earlier, at the Maryknoll language school in Bolivia, Henri had met Fr. John Vesey, an American diocesan priest and missionary. "Since 1972, John has been a good friend even though we did not see much of each other…friendship was emerging as an important part of my own vocation as a priest," explained Henri. He saw John Vesey as "a friend who would be there at crucial moments."[43] This was another of those moments.

In August 1984, Henri flew to join John Vesey in Guatemala, a country that still saw little sign of resolution to a civil war that began there in 1960 and that would continue until the year after Henri died. "I will never forget the moment the road made a turn and opened up a spectacular view of Lake Atitlán, surrounded by volcanoes wrapped with fast-moving clouds, and decorated on its edges with small towns shining like jewels on a golden ring."[44] As Henri admired this picturesque backdrop, Vesey told him about the "large cell blocks in the capital city where people torture people day and night with the most sophisticated methods available. Thousands of Guatemalan Indians are being tortured and killed in a systematic attempt to silence the voices crying out for justice and peace."[45]

Henri's short visit to war-torn Guatemala in 1984 resulted in *Love in a Fearful Land: A Guatemala Story.* He was clearly conflicted by what he saw. He watched the Brooklyn-born, no-nonsense John Vesey at work in the *favelas* of Santiago Atitlán and saw an inspiring missionary priest in action: "He jokes, laughs, and teases whenever he has a chance. He hides little and shows his heart to anyone who wants to see it. Yet all of this belongs to his prayer. Prayer is living in unceasing communion with God and God's people.… Prayer is living in in the heart of God—a heart of justice, peace, and righteousness."[46]

He also felt helpless. "I saw the lack of material resources, education, and medical care, and responded first with a strong desire to do something about it all. But I discovered quickly that this mindset is like that of the problem solver with all the 'know how'.... When our main motivation is to bring about successful changes, we may in the long run do more harm than good, because the urge to bring about change often carried violence in its wake."[47]

Henri is aware he is caught in a paradox. "Somehow it seems hard for us to truly believe that God loves the people of Central and South America as much as he loves us, and that his love is as fruitful there as anywhere else."[48] Today, had Henri been able to return to Guatemala he would learn that forensic anthropologists are still at work at sites across the country dealing with the consequences of Guatemala's horrifying unfinished business. Their task is to identify the bones of the disappeared—those who were murdered, many of them indigenous people, during the war that continued until 1996. They use DNA swabs taken from living relatives. Fredy Peccerelli is the founder of Guatemala's Foundation for Forensic Anthropology (*Fundación de Antropología Forense de Guatemala*). In March 2012, he met the sister of Hugo Navarro, an activist who disappeared in 1984. He told her, "'We've found your brother, we have his body.' I was quite pleased with all the information I was giving her but then she turned to me and said, 'Thank you, and my son? He disappeared as well, haven't you found him?' I fell apart. I thought we'd achieved something great, and perhaps it was, but it wasn't everything."[49]

Back in 1984, during their conversations, Vesey brought up the idea that Henri might write a book about what he had witnessed in Guatemala. Perhaps this book could include the story of Fr. Stanley Rother, the missionary priest from Oklahoma who had been murdered by a gun squad in 1981 in the room they now used as their chapel at Santiago Atitlán? Vesey was shocked by what he learned. "This gifted writer told me that he had not been able to write anything for over a year and a half. I had asked him to do something that he was unable to do, and with my request, his cross only grew heavier."[50]

Henri left Guatemala to visit another mentor he felt he needed to consult. Jean Vanier and Henri Nouwen would seem like natural colleagues, both innovative and influential through their work and their books. They more or less stumbled into each other's orbits. Vanier read widely and had noted that Henri had mentioned L'Arche in his books. He identified Nouwen as someone of interest and had invited him to travel from Harvard to give a L'Arche retreat in Chicago. At that event, Jean thought that Henri might benefit from a closer look at L'Arche and asked him to consider visiting L'Arche in France, not to give another keynote address, but simply to spend time there and to observe. Henri was certainly interested in the opportunity of talking with Vanier, someone whose books he had read and who had the potential to become a mentor. Behind this invitation perhaps Vanier saw the possibility of a longer-term commitment. Henri took up Vanier's offer. He had organized his Harvard schedule to allow for extended breaks between courses, and this one enabled him to fly to France and visit Trosly-Breuil, the village about an hour's drive north and slightly east of Paris. This is where L'Arche began, and Henri wanted to know more about the man Jean Vanier and what he was actually doing there.

The journey to Trosly-Breuil takes you through the center of the old city of Compiègne at the edge of a large forest. As you leave the town behind to get to the village, you pass a strange sight on the left. It's a solitary railcar with great historic significance. This is the *Wagon de l'Armistice*, the railcar in which the defeated German army signed the document in November 1918 to bring an end to the First World War at the eleventh hour of the eleventh day of the eleventh month. The railcar was turned into a museum because of its historic importance. Then in 1940, in a cynical piece of state-theater, Adolf Hitler demanded that this same railcar be used as the setting for the defeated French government to sign the document of surrender, formalizing the German occupation of France.

Henri was not there to visit historic sites. He continued up the road for another fifteen minutes to Trosly-Breuil. When Henri arrived, Vanier could see that he was in a state of personal confusion and not working from a clear plan. "I think Henri is someone who doesn't look that far ahead," his Canadian host later recalled.

> He's an "of the moment" day-to-day person. I think he was essentially yearning for relationships, meeting new people, and yearning for deeper, permanent relationships. So I think coming here was also about being able to meet with me as much as he could, but being at L'Arche, maybe it was also about bringing two realities together. Something about discovering the meaning of community, about being in a community, experiencing community life, and seeing L'Arche maybe as a vision for the future, for the church. But I think it was also a desire to get to know me better.

Vanier could see that Henri was suffering, but he was uncertain about the kind of role he was being expected to play. Although Henri was only four years younger, perhaps he was looking for Vanier to be the older brother he had never had. Maybe Henri thought of him as another kind of father figure. Whatever was the case, Vanier could see that Henri needed help. "I realized it had to be about more than Harvard. I felt that for Henri L'Arche was his potential salvation, but from what I didn't know. There would be no expectations on our part, nor need there be any on his—he'd have a nice room, plenty of time to write. He would also have occasion to meet me."

Also visiting L'Arche at that time was David Perrin, a seminarian from Canada who was taking a break from his studies at the Pontifical Gregorian University in Rome. He had applied to work as a volunteer at L'Arche between his courses. Jean's mother, Pauline Vanier—always referred to as "Madame Vanier" since her husband, Georges, had been Canada's Governor General from 1959 to 1967—was living at Trosly at the time. She invited this young Canadian visitor for tea and cookies at her cottage, and these tea breaks became their daily routine. "It was here, at these tea-times, where I met Henri Nouwen," Perrin explains. "I don't remember us talking about much of any consequence but what I do remember is that 'tea-time' was pleasant and meaningful—and we used real tea cups with saucers! Madame Vanier kept the tea and cookies replenished and the three of us got on rather well—chatting, sitting comfortably, informally visiting."

It was in the silence of the simple barn-like chapel at Trosly that David discovered more:

> I remember the chapel was rather ill-lit, but there was always some natural light. As a result I remember it as being a room of shadows, especially where the Blessed Sacrament was kept. Most days I would go to the chapel either in the morning or evening when I did not have other responsibilities to spend some time in silence before the Blessed Sacrament. As I entered the chapel I would

frequently encounter Henri prostrate on the floor, face down, head buried in his folded arms, in prayer before the Blessed Sacrament. He would scarcely move, ever. I sat in a chair close-by since the space was not that large. Rarely would there be other people around. My time of silence would normally not last beyond forty-five minutes or an hour but Henri would be there often before and often after my own time. My assumption was that he would spend great lengths of time in this prostrate position, in silence, in prayer, in contemplation. This was something we never talked about during our tea-time chats. He may not even have known that it was me sitting in the background—some "body" occasionally shifting weight and interrupting the silence with the inevitable creak of the chair upon which I sat.

Eventually, David Perrin returned to his studies in Rome and was ordained,[51] and Henri received a letter from Joe Egan, the Director of Daybreak, the L'Arche community in Richmond Hill in Ontario.

CHAPTER FOUR

FINDING SHELTER IN THE ARK

{ 1985–1991 }

"…complicated, wonderful, and terrible…"

He was on sabbatical in France, in L'Arche," explains Sr. Sue Mosteller, a member of the Sisters of St. Joseph and also the team at Daybreak. "I said 'What are you doing next year?' He said, 'I don't know, I have no idea, but I know I'm not going back to Harvard.'"

Henri the priest-writer-professor had had enough of that final hyphen. He was disillusioned by university culture. "One of the saddest aspects of the lives of many students is that they always feel pressured.… Books written to be savored slowly are read hastily to fulfill requirements, paintings made to be seen with a contemplative eye are taken in as part of a necessary art appreciation course, and music composed to be enjoyed at leisure is listened to in order to identify a period or style. Thus, colleges and universities meant to be places for quiet learning have become places of fierce competition, in which the rewards go to those who produce the most and the best."[1]

It was with these thoughts about leaving the competitive world of Ivy League academia behind that he continued to listen to what Sue Mosteller had to say.

> So I began to tell him about Daybreak and what we were planning. I said, "Well, we always say we are going to talk about spirituality here, and it's complicated and wonderful and terrible," I said. "We do have this dream that we can

become a community that is a really solid spiritual base with solid theology, and not kooky theology." He was so interested and was so alive during that conversation.

After a ten-day initial visit to Daybreak, Henri made a decision about the invitation in Joe Egan's letter. He would enter daily life in a L'Arche community at a time when the organization had accumulated more than twenty years of adaptation and development following Jean Vanier's first attempt at building community with people living with disabilities. Starting with that single *foyer* in 1964, by the time Henri joined the Daybreak community in Ontario, L'Arche was already operating in sixteen countries. By comparison, today L'Arche has a hundred and forty-nine communities in thirty-eight countries around the world.[2] Each is built on the same approach that Jean Vanier initiated in 1964 with Raphaël Simi and Philippe Seux: to create a welcoming home (a *foyer* or hearth) for people (known as "core members") with intellectual and developmental disabilities in order that they might live together in small family communities. Core members live with assistants, who are not specialists but often people who are young and from around the world who seek this model of community life. As Vanier said about L'Arche in a recent newspaper interview, "I wanted to build a community and not an institution."[3]

When Henri entered daily life in a L'Arche community, he was experiencing the accumulation of more than twenty years of adaptation and development of Vanier's ideas about inclusive and transformational community building.

Henri felt finally ready to make the break with Harvard and academic life. He moved to Daybreak, the first Canadian L'Arche community, founded in 1969, in Richmond Hill, Ontario, a forty-minute drive north of Toronto. Arriving there in 1986 to work as its pastor, Henri would report to Joe Egan, the director, and work closely with Sue Mosteller.

Henri began his Daybreak years in the first and largest L'Arche community in Canada. The Daybreak he arrived at was very different from the Daybreak of today. In 1986 it was a collection of fourteen scattered homes split between Richmond Hill and Toronto. After driving north and turning off the busy north-south highway, Henri would enter the large rural campus in Richmond Hill that is enclosed within rough-hewn and wind-worn wooden fences. He might have thought at first that he was moving in to a farm, especially with the tall barn that housed the carpentry shop—the Woodery. He would have to look carefully to see the two original *foyers*, or homes, and the workshops dotted throughout the property behind trees in this rolling stretch of grassy land about an hour's drive north of Toronto. Today there are eight *foyers*. Then, in addition to the two on the rural site, there were more *foyers* in the town of Richmond Hill, and also in Toronto. Urban or rural, each *foyer* was (and is today) home to a mixed group of five to seven core members and assistants. In the 1990s, Daybreak Richmond Hill and L'Arche Toronto became two separate entities, but when Henri first arrived they were one and the same. In Richmond Hill, then as today, there is an obvious center to the place: the Meeting Hall, for day programs and larger gatherings. In 1986, the chapel was in Toronto and more than a decade later, in Richmond Hill, a new angular wood-framed chapel with its steeply sloping roof was built beside a small pond. This was a chapel that Henri would never use.

Nathan Ball began working at Daybreak around the same time as Henri. He says it was a death in the family that brought him to L'Arche. A recent graduate from the University of Waterloo,

Nathan had returned to live with his family in western Canada when, unexpectedly, his youngest brother became ill and died.

> He had lived with several disabilities, particularly in the later part of his life and around the same time I met a wise elder from the L'Arche community who said to me, "If you want to understand more about what you have lived with your brother, why don't you consider spending time in L'Arche?" So I did, and I never left.

To walk into a L'Arche event or home can be challenging if you have not spent much time in the company of people with intellectual or developmental difficulties. Nathan Ball summarizes what Henri would have seen when he walked into any of the Daybreak homes.

> You'd knock on the door just like you would to go to any home. Someone would open the door and welcome you in. If you were there to stay for a few hours you would experience warm and very normal, everyday relationships between people with disabilities and young assistants. Cooking, cleaning, sharing their meals together, talking, laughing, conflicts.

One of the initial challenges for Henri would be language, in the sense that it takes time for a newcomer to be able to interpret clearly what people are saying. Some disabilities make it difficult for people to move their vocal or facial muscles. Listening from a pastoral perspective had always been easy for Henri, but this would be quite a different and intense hearing test for him.

Ball explains that he met Henri the previous winter in Trosly-Breuil and was not especially confident about this famous author's ability to adjust to life in a L'Arche community. "Henri had a fair bit of difficulty managing, I would say living, in the physical world. He was awkward. He didn't know how to cook. He fumbled. He was much more at ease in the world of ideas and intellect and I say in the world of the heart, in the world of compassion and of caring and of teaching. So the day-to-day life of the L'Arche community was very confusing for him at times."

Henri often confused his colleagues in return, as Sue Mosteller experienced:

> He'd be telling me about this book that he read, very excited about the concepts and the thoughts and every-thing, and I'm saying "Yes! Yes!" and "Oh, that's so good!" Then he'd leave quickly because he was always going to something else, and then all day long I'd be grinding with this thing in my head, inside myself, saying "Oh yeah, well that fits with that. Oh yeah." Then the next day I'd say, "You know about that book, I wanted to say…" and he'd say "Huh?" He was gone from there and on to some-thing else now and he'd say, "I want to tell you all about this other person I met who had this to say and now let's talk about that." So I could never catch up.

After four years of this new way of life at Daybreak, Henri was out walking one day and was hit by a passing car. He needed urgent surgery to remove his damaged spleen. This was a real brush with death that led him "to a new experience of God," he said, and the realization that "the interruptions to [his] everyday life…have most revealed to [him] the divine mystery of which [he is] a part."[4]

Relieved that Henri had survived the accident, Ball could see that he was someone dealing with a lot of unresolved tensions. He thought that this was because of Henri's desire to find a new way of teaching and preaching and being present to the larger world. He wanted to get off the circuit and find a new context. But there was a very deep personal reason for his coming to L'Arche and that was finding a home for his restless heart. And he found that, partly, in the context of the family quality of L'Arche. In a way, when Henri landed in L'Arche Daybreak, he jumped into the deep end of a very big swimming pool and he wasn't a good swimmer.

Nathan Ball thinks that Henri's real breakthrough at Daybreak came during the first year he arrived. He was asked to take care of Adam Arnett, a twenty-five-year-old core member. It was Henri's job to bathe, shave, dress, and serve Adam breakfast. Because of so many seizures as a child, Adam could not speak and was so physically disabled that this morning routine took two hours. "I began with fear and trembling.... I didn't want to be a source of embarrassment…I have no idea whether Adam had confidence in me or not," Henri later wrote in his famous book about Adam.[5]

The morning routine with Adam challenged and changed Henri profoundly. "The tables were turning. Adam was becoming *my* teacher, taking me by the hand, walking with me in my confusion through the wilderness of *my* life.... We were friends, brothers, bonded in our hearts."[6]

Although Adam could not speak about it, his other assistants could see that his relationship with Henri was especially meaningful, and he was very aware whenever Henri was not there with him. The assistants put a photograph of Henri in Adam's room so he could still see Henri even when he was away teaching or giving a retreat. In the many of the photographs of Henri and Adam in that room, you can clearly see Henri's framed portrait in the background.

Even in his silence, Adam influenced the way Henri wrote, as his friend and editor at Orbis Books, Robert Ellsberg, discovered. "I think the books achieved more and more depth and authenticity as he lived that out more authentically in his last ten years." For example, Henri proposed writing a book about the Apostle's Creed, but it was the experience of living with Adam that inspired Henri to modify his ideas for the book. Robert saw that caring for Adam had become such an important spiritual experience for Henri that "often in his talks, on any topic, he would often use Adam as the central motif to talk about peace making or the Gospel or what it means to be beloved of God because he had discovered, through this mute helpless man, a sense that we have a mission and a value and an identity in the eyes of God that has nothing to do with being famous writers or swift athletes or anything like that. I think that it had been an experience of deep conversion for him. He felt that it was one of the most important spiritual relationships that he had developed, or experienced, caring for this Adam."

That experience shaped a different kind of book about the Apostle's Creed: *Adam: God's Beloved*, as Ellsberg explains.

> He told the story of Adam as a kind of figure for the story of Christ, as a kind of Way of the Cross through the life of Adam. It was quite remarkable and it really was Henri's Creed. It was a summary of everything he'd learned, a synthesis of everything that had converged in his experience at L'Arche that would have taught him about the Gospel, about what it means to be a child of God.

The book was published shortly after Henri died. In those final years of increasing international celebrity in publishing, giving retreats, and keynote addresses at conferences, Henri was living under intense pressure. The members of the Daybreak community were concerned about what these seemingly endless demands were doing to him. Nathan Ball says that Henri was highly ambivalent about this celebrity status:

> On the one hand he wanted for all the right reasons to be able to share with a large group of people the insight and the wisdom and the passion that he had about the spiritual life and the bigger the platform the better. Standing in front of a hundred people, or a thousand people, or five thousand people who are looking up at you with adoring eyes is a powerful affective experience. So it was compelling for him from that perspective. However, he had this growing experience that being in front of a big group, being the person of interest, being the one who attracted the television cameras, in the end, left him with an experience of emptiness. I would say that was untenable for him. He wanted the interest and he wanted the attention. On the other hand, that's not *really* what he wanted.

Ball then returns to the image of Daybreak as a dangerous swimming pool:

> It was a pool of water that was much safer than the celebrity status that he was trying to move away from. Now he didn't leave it entirely and he became a celebrity at Daybreak too. He needed that and wanted that, so he was conflicted. He was ambivalent. He was impossible to support sometimes. He would often come to two or three of us and say, "I've got twenty-five invitations, help me decide what I should say yes to and what I should say no to." He listened to some of what we said. He wanted to live a quieter life, a simpler life, and yet he was running away from it at the same time.

Henri had some serious unfinished business to attend to. Reading the books that will not appear until after his death reveals the combustible elements of a profound crisis that he was confronting. Some who were close to Henri sensed them. Others would be surprised by what they later learned. Within two years of living at Daybreak, Henri writes, "I had at one time become totally dependent on the affection and friendship of one person. This dependency threw me into a pit of great anguish and brought me to the verge of a very self-destructive depression."[7] With a telling point-counterpoint observation about depression, Andrew Solomon, professor of clinical psychology at the Columbia University Medical Center, writes, "Life events are often triggers of depression" and a few lines later, "what remains unclear is when depression triggers life events."[8] Henri seemed caught between the two.

His dependency focused on Nathan Ball.

> It became clear as we, as our relationship evolved, that there was a sense in which Henri was depending on me to help him find his place of belonging in the world and I wasn't unhappy to have a role in that, but as the expectations became more than I could fulfil, as it were, I realized that this image of "lifeguard" wasn't going to work. That wasn't something I could do or fulfil.

Henri fell apart. "I experienced a very concrete break with my best friend. At that moment my whole world came crashing down and it seemed as though all the losses of my whole life came back to haunt me."[9]

Richard Sipe, Henri's colleague at the Menninger Foundation, looks back on this time in Henri's life with a clinical and also a pastoral eye. He distinguishes between things that are individual to Henri and things that he considers are part of the clerical culture that had influenced him so powerfully. "Henri did struggle with depression, and I think part of his depression was over his sexual loneliness, his sexual unsolved problem." After leaving religious life, Sipe continued his research into celibacy and formation in religious life.

> Now, many of us, we fall in love in that way when we're teenagers and we kind of let go and idealize this woman or we idealize this man, this person, whom we think should be a friend, a very close friend. Henri had not gone through that stage, and he knew it. I had written about this, that the Catholic priesthood fosters prolonged adolescence in people, the dependency and the idealization, and so on, and I think he knew that. Here's Henri, after twenty-five years in the priesthood, for the first time allowing himself the human feelings of falling in love. In his case, he fell in love with a man, which was appropriate to his orientation. It brought things, unfinished problems, to the fore.

In the midst of his crisis Henri wrote, "My dark side says: 'I am no good.... I deserve to be pushed aside, forgotten, rejected, and abandoned.'"[10] He sought professional help and, from December 1987 to June 1988, Henri moved to a counseling center in Winnipeg, Manitoba.

The Jungian psychologist, James Hillman, wrote that it is through depression that "we enter depths and in depth find soul. Depression is essential to the tragic sense of life. It moistens the dry soul, and dries the wet. It brings refuge, limitation, focus, gravity, weight, and humble powerlessness. It reminds of death."[11]

Henri's time in counseling in Winnipeg would be as difficult as it was intense. Through his training in psychology he would know, as Andrew Solomon summarizes, that major depression

> has a number of defining factors, mostly having to do
> with withdrawal, though agitated or atypical depres-
> sion may have an intense negativity rather than a flat-
> tened passivity—and is usually fairly easy to recognize; it
> deranges sleep, appetites, and energy. It tends to increase
> sensitivity to rejection, and it may be accompanied by a
> loss of self-confidence and self-regard.[12]

The Oblate priest Ronald Rolheiser, author of *The Holy Longing: The Search for a Christian Spirituality*, recalled meeting Henri when he was staying in Winnipeg. They found themselves presenting talks at a conference for members of Catholic school boards in Canada. One of the keynote speakers had dropped out at the last minute, and one of the organizers knew that Henri happened to be in Winnipeg and invited him to speak, unannounced, at the last minute. "I didn't know till after, reading his books, that he was there because he was in a depression," says Rolheiser.

> I was taken by his depth, but also at the time there was
> a humorlessness. I couldn't have described it at the time,
> but there was a depression in him. He didn't fill the room
> with energy when you were with him alone. It's inter-
> esting when he was in public, when he spoke, he was high
> energy. He blew the people away. The irony is that most
> of them didn't know who he was. They thought he was a
> substitute speaker.

This was Rolheiser's first meeting with the famous Henri Nouwen, and he admits to being a little starstruck. "It was kind of, this is my hero. Wow!" The difference between the public and the private Henri was very noticeable.

He looked at you. He connected. He was very warm, but at the time I didn't know he was basically inside of a clinical depression. I wouldn't have described it like that. I just thought, well, maybe that's his depth. The interesting thing was the contrast between his stage persona. He just set up a chair. He sat on the edge and you kind of had a chat with him. With his perpetual scarf! He just picked up the microphone—and this was a big audience, hundreds of people—and he just wowed them. Then he'd come off it. It wasn't like he sobbed or something, but the energy just drained from him.

When Richard Sipe met Henri on a retreat in 1991, Henri told him of his plans to turn the private journal he had kept in Winnipeg into a book. "Really, he was frank about it, and he's written about it, of course, that he had a breakdown. He said he kept notes during that time and he wondered whether he should publish those. We talked about it, and I said yes, I thought it would be helpful to a lot of people."

Not published until 1996, *The Inner Voice of Love: A Journey Through Anguish to Freedom* takes the form of affirmations and statements written by someone in the midst of great distress. "Stop being a pleaser."[13] "Simply start by admitting that you cannot cure yourself."[14] "Your deepest, truest self is not yet home."[15] Toward the end of these reflections he returns to the central theme of his hugely successful 1992 book about a father and his sons that we will turn to later. "Be gentle with yourself, and let your heart be your loving parent as you live your wounds through."[16]

Sipe reflected on the enormous difficulties of living the vowed life of a celibate priest, especially when that decision was made by a six-year-old who is now well into midlife:

I think he was a lonely man, but the spiritual life and the priesthood is a lonely life. It's a life that St. Augustine talked about, the loneliness, the long loneliness of life—"Lord, late have I loved thee / Oh beauty ever ancient, ever new"—that sense of coming to things late, or having missed certain things, or having certain regrets. I don't think that's contrary to the spiritual life. You know, it was very interesting that when Henri and I said goodbye after our retreat, I did something very uncharacteristic of me at the time. I hugged and I kissed Henri. That wouldn't have been common to me, and I thought about it afterwards. I said to Henri something that I wouldn't have ordinarily said at that time. I said, "I love you." It was, in a sense, the right thing to do. Afterwards, I thought I was instinctively responding in a very human way to Henri and his loneliness and what he needed from people. He needed warmth, and he needed the assurance of love.

After six months in Winnipeg, Henri returned to the place of nourishment he thought of as home: Daybreak, "the place of light, the place of truth, the place of love."[17]

CHAPTER FIVE

An Unfinished Book

❴ 1991–1995 ❵

"That little event had many consequences for me."

Carolyn Whitney-Brown recalls her first and terrifying meeting with Henri. She and her husband, Geoff, were contemplating becoming assistants at Daybreak. Both had graduate degrees in literature, missionary experience in Africa, and backgrounds in Ignatian spirituality. They were also raising a young family. Henri drove Carolyn and Geoff to lunch at a pizza restaurant not far from Daybreak. It's the driving that she remembers most.

> It was after his accident when he was hit by the mirror of the van and almost died. So he crammed us into his little car and went off to lunch and he drives wanting eye contact with his passenger. He's far more interested in eye-contact with this passenger than with the road and he was explaining to me—I remember clearly—how after his accident, before he went into surgery he really made his peace with life and his peace with the world, and was really so sad to find he had survived. But no one understood that—or few people understood that having made his peace, we would have been happy not to have to pick up the mess of his life again and start making mistakes again. We were careening along the road, and he wasn't watching the road, he was explaining those things to me and I actually got in touch with the profound desire to live within myself at that moment.

Fortunately, the Whitney-Browns survived the journey, as well as the lunch.

We made it safely to the Pizza Barrel, where we settled in and he sat there and he took off his glasses. He kind of mushed his face around, wrapped his elbows around each other, and just told us what a mess he felt like he was, and how he became more handicapped all the time and how lonely, and all. The waitress was very kind to him. I think she was used to him. I remember that when his glass ran out of coke or something, he picked up his empty glass and kind of trailed around the restaurant, following the waitress. He forgot that you summon the waitress to you and she was saying, "Sit down, Henri. It's okay."

The Whitney-Browns moved to Daybreak in 1990, working there until 1997, and they got to know Henri very well.

Henri fit very well into L'Arche. Henri was wounded and handicapped himself. He needed affirmation. He wanted to know he was loved. It was as simple as any other human being. He wanted to know that he was valued for who he was, not for what he did, not for what he wrote, but people knew him and loved him himself. In that way it was an excellent fit for Henri. People loved him on his own terms and they really got to know him and offered him a kind of unconditional love that I don't think he would have found anywhere else.

In the fall of 1991 Henri took a L'Arche equivalent of a sabbatical and returned once more to Europe to spend some time with his father. They traveled to Freiburg in Germany and visited the cathedral, "one of the best places to see in stone the place where power and piety meet," as Henri noted.[1] Another reason for the trip was for Henri to meet with staff at Herder, his German publisher. Performing in Freiburg that week was Circus Barum, a large traveling circus. One of the featured acts was the Flying Rodleighs, and the two Nouwens, *vader en zoon*, decided to go and see it. "That little event had many consequences for me," Henri would later write in his diary. [2] "I was 'hooked' by the Rodleighs and felt nearly driven to see them again and again and enter deeply into their world."[3]

Rodleigh Stevens is a fifth-generation circus artist originally from South Africa, and he remembers fondly the stranger who insisted on finding out all he could about his troupe, the Flying Rodleighs. It was a first encounter that he says became "a turning point in our lives." Henri met with them several times in the few remaining years in his life and even followed them on the road for several weeks. That first meeting was, says Rodleigh, "a very unusual encounter. Straight after our performance he came backstage, which was the traditional time for us to talk about the performance. Henri loved those discussions. He loved those interactions." But he was disruptive. "After a while it started to become a bit annoying to us, to say, 'Who is this old guy and why is he in our faces all the time?'"

In their sequined form-fitting outfits, the Rodleighs were not always clear about what was going on, but they soon learned that Henri never ran out of questions, "and we just had to answer them, and he was never satisfied with just any particular answer. It had to be detailed. He was quite tenacious with getting that information."

They decided to invite him to watch them in rehearsal, perhaps assuming that would be the end of it. The team grew increasingly more curious as Henri "became quite obsessed with the technicalities of the flying trapeze, our lifestyle, how we did things, why we did things."

Rodleigh says that Henri "regarded the whole team as his friend," and as a team they did what performing artists do for serious fans: they put on a private show and dragged him into it. During a practice session they rigged Henri in safety lines and got him up on the pole from which he could reach the trapeze, swing on it, and then drop safely to the net.

> After he landed in the net, he lay there for about two or three minutes, with this enormous smile on his face. He just lay there in silence. He didn't mutter a word. He didn't say anything. It was like adrenaline had taken over his whole body and he was frozen in the moment and he just lay there, looking up with this enormous grin on his face. He finally turned to us and said, "That was wonderful!"[4]

They would learn even more about this priest who never stopped asking them questions when they attended his funeral.

Back at Daybreak, Nathan Ball understood Henri's interest in the circus:

> I do think the physicality of it was very interesting to him and compelling for him. This was dance, this was theatre on the big stage and he was an artist. He was very drawn to this. He wanted to travel with them and get to know how they related and what their struggles were and what made a good day and what made a bad day, and he wanted to get right inside of that experience. He did see, very quickly I think, that this trapeze was a metaphor for the spiritual life. There is a catcher, and the spiritual life is about letting yourself be caught by the catcher.

Henri discovered something very powerful the instant he saw the Flying Rodleighs perform. Was this some kind of mystical revelation under the big top? Perhaps. What is beyond speculation, though, is that what fell into place at that moment would take a book for Henri to explain it adequately. He was clear on the metaphor but wanted all the technical details about how the team worked and communicated with each other as they performed. He needed information about the ropes, nets, timing, flying, and, especially, catching. He would be as precise about their physical actions as he was about the spiritual interpretation he was attaching to them. He was being the kind of journalist he so admired in Thomas Merton. Although sketched out, his book about the theology of the flyer and the catcher remains another piece of Henri's unfinished business.

Earlier, in 1978, Henri had introduced the circus metaphor into his writing, one that identified clowns as those who offer "consolation, comfort, hope, and a smile" in between the "frightening acts of heroes." The world needs more clowns, he says, because they are "people who by their empty, solitary lives of inner communion with the God who dwells within speak to our 'other side.'"[5] Clowns "remind us of what happens between the scenes. The clowns show us by their 'useless' behaviour not simply that many of our preoccupations, worries, tension, and anxieties need a smile, but that we too have white on our faces and that we too are called to clown a little."[6] Where there are clowns, there are always tears.

It was in 1995, during another sabbatical, when Henri received the telephone call informing him that Adam Arnett, now thirty-four, was not doing well. Henri returned to Daybreak in Ontario for what would be the final days of Adam's life. Carolyn Whitney-Brown touches on a sensitive tension point about Henri's relationship with Adam when she reflects on how, sometimes, Henri could "write about him more than he was spending time with him. Then he'd have to come back and kind of regroup himself to be with Adam, having ventured off into writing about him without actually being in the presence of Adam himself." This was different. Henri would be there for Adam, his family, and his Daybreak community.

"When I walked into Adam's hospital room," explained Henri, "I was deeply moved to see my dear friend lying there, obviously living his final hours with us. I kissed him on the forehead and stroked his hair. Although his eyes were open, I wasn't certain whether he recognized me."[7]

Adam was struggling to breathe, and the prognosis was not good. "I anointed Adam's forehead and both his hands, asking God to give him all the inner strength he needed to make his final passage."[8] The doctors removed the life-support devices and later that night Adam died, with his grief-filled parents by his side.

Henri officiated at the funeral. It was an event with a huge impact for the entire Daybreak community, as Whitney-Brown explains: "Adam's funeral was the most remarkable thing, though, because Henri said so truthfully that he saw in Adam something of what it must have been to be near Jesus. That everyone who touched him was healed, it says in the Gospels. People came from all over the world to the funeral of this man who never spoke, to say that in some way, by touching him, it had been healing in their lives. Henri named that, really accurately, that people's experience of Adam was profoundly healing."

In Henri's words: "His great teaching to us was, 'I can live only if you surround me with love and if you love one another. Otherwise, my life is useless and I am a burden.'"[9] To meet Adam was to encounter "a love turned to grief, soaked in tears, and full of longing."[10]

Henri had been at Daybreak for almost a decade now and it was clearly time for a performance review. Henri called this his "discernment process." As Whitney-Brown explains, it was a process intended to help the ever-restless Henri decide if Daybreak "was a good fit, whether the way he lived in community was healthy, good for him, good for the community, and how the next few years would look like."

Daybreak arranged for Jean Vanier to come over from France and also invited priests from affiliated churches to come and interview the resident community. "So they spent, I think, about a week touring around and talking to us all about Henri. The whole community was a hotbed of Henri stories, and peopled discussing Henri and thinking about Henri." Inevitably, anecdotes surfaced about how difficult life with Nouwen could be.

> There were struggles with Henri in the community. People sometimes warped their lives out of shape so he wouldn't feel disappointed. But the gifts he brought, of celebration and joy and energy, and bringing in the outside world! Also, we noted that around the tables that week, as people were discussing Henri and Henri stories, the laughter was unbelievable. Henri was very eccentric and fun, and Jean had this inspiration. He said, "Let's do skits tonight at the finale of this week of discernment."

And they did, even though this finale event was to be open to the public and attended by a Roman Catholic archbishop, an Anglican bishop, a representative from the national office of the United Church of Canada, and various other distinguished visitors. Whitney-Brown recalls:

There was a skit of Henri and his secretary, with him slowly having a kind of breakdown of anxiety and her recommending that he read his books because he might find them helpful. There was a skit where someone dressed as Henri ran around waving their arms, pretending to give a homily and practically lighting the edge of their cassock on fire while people ran behind him to move the candles. I wrote a version of "The Man on the Flying Trapeze" that we sang with just as much musical skill as we usually sing at L'Arche.

This could easily have gone embarrassingly wrong, but as the evening progressed, Jean Vanier watched Henri's reactions closely and could see how delighted he was by what was being said, as did Carolyn. "The visiting dignitaries forgot they were dignified and laughed. It was a good evening and Henri thanked us," she says. When the skits were over, "standing out under the stars" as she notes, they loaded Henri's car with the candles and props to drive the short distance back to the chapel where they were stored.

Henri looked at us with marvel, and said, "I didn't know you knew me so well." It was the best line of the evening. Of course! Everybody knew him well. You couldn't live with Henri and not know him well, but it was Jean's brilliance to recognize that Henri wouldn't know that we loved him well if we just told him that. We had to demonstrate that we really did know him and loved him and wanted to live with him.

What about those eccentricities that seemed to be of concern to Henri?

We understood them, really well, better than Henri himself did in some ways. They were lovable to his community. I think in that moment he really got some-thing deep, received it deeply that he was loved. It's a story as much about Jean Vanier's wisdom, to recognize that this event was a way for Henri to really feel, on a heart level, on a gut level, that this could be his home.

And for a little longer, that's what Daybreak was.

CHAPTER SIX

A PRODIGAL SON RETURNS

❴ 1995–1996 ❵

*"What is meant and represented here is the divine love and mercy in
its power to transform Death into Life."*

Leave is a privilege, not a right," states the Yale faculty hand-book.[1] The Harvard faculty handbook says: "Ordinarily, faculty members should not be out of the Harvard classroom for more than a year at a time."[2] Throughout his teaching life, Henri arranged for frequent breaks between his courses and commitments. He clearly knew how to negotiate a contract and Daybreak's was no different. On Saturday, September 2, 1995, he wrote in his diary, "This is the first day of my sabbatical. I am excited and anxious, hopeful and fearful, tired, and full of desire to do a thousand things."[3] One of the thousand things was a visit to his father. "The first thing my ninety-three-year-old father said," notes Henri, "was, 'Well, you badly need a haircut.'… A father is always a father."[4] Henri recognizes a familiar pattern, "I still wanted to change my father, hoping that he would give me the kind of attention I desired."[5]

Within months, the tone has changed. "Deep within myself I feel that something new wants to be born…. There is a sense of conclusion and new beginnings. This sabbatical year seems to be the year of transition from an active traveling life to a life of contemplation and writing."[6]

Henri's brother, Laurent, explains that this certainly made it feel like a different kind of visit. Henri told him he was about to ask for nothing less than "the ultimate blessing" from their father. He decided that the best moment to do this would be on one of their annual visits to a monastery.

Henri went that summer to a monastery with my father, in the south of Belgium. My father at that time was ninety-three and Henri was sixty-three, and they drove down there by car. It was very funny because Henri wanted to drive and my father didn't want to commit suicide with Henri next to him! So there was competition. For my father to drive at ninety-three was also a dangerous situation. But they drove there, on the highways, and they got there. Well, maybe after such an experience they needed to talk to each other! And they did. They had a good conversation. My father asked Henri for forgiveness for what he had been and Henri asked my father for forgiveness.

Henri was so moved by this intimate conversation with his father that he telephoned his phenomenological psychology friend from his Nijmegen University days, Peter Naus. Then at St. Jerome's University in Ontario, Naus was doing research into the experience and meaning of being blessed by one's father, research that Henri knew about.

Henri called me and said, "Peter, I want you to know that my father blessed me." I said, "Tell me," and he said, "We had a family dinner and my father said," and now I have to paraphrase, "I would like to say something to Henri because I understand that Henri has wondered about whether I love and appreciate him. Henri, I want you to know I love you and I am proud of you." There was definitely more closeness between Henri and his father near the end of his life than there was before, but it was a complex relationship for most of his life.

It would have been very interesting to be in the backseat of that car listening to this recently and newly reconciled father and son as Henri drove them back home from Belgium. Perhaps they sang old folksongs in Dutch. Perhaps they made that journey in complete silence. We'll never know now. But for Henri, it does seem to have brought him to something like the completion of a piece of unfinished business that had been nagging away at him for so many years.

His brother Laurent certainly noticed something different.

> They did reconcile at the very end, in a certain way. Saying this, I do realize that for all people, the relationship with their father and with their mother is always a relationship with tensions. These can be negative, they can be positive. That certainly was the situation for Henri, but he worked it out at the very last days of his life, together with my father, in his very last days.

Of course, Henri was not to know that this visit had anything to do with his own last days. This was, for him, another brief family excursion at the start of a busy sabbatical year and the prelude to a major project with a Dutch television company requiring a film shoot in St. Petersburg. That would be next. Henri's 1992 book, *The Return of the Prodigal Son*, remained a bestseller and was now available in many languages. Given its popularity, Henri had been invited by a television producer, Jan van den Bosch, to participate in a documentary about Rembrandt's painting, the parable, and in which he wanted to feature Henri's insights. The idea was to take him to the Hermitage Museum where he would explain, on camera, what he could see in the famous painting and how his thoughts about it had continued to evolve since the book was first released. The recent visit with his father offered him even more material to consider using in the film, no doubt.

Henri's first encounter with this painting by Rembrandt was, like seeing the Flying Rodleighs perform, a chance discovery with profound life-changing consequences. In 1983, during that particularly dark time, when he was struggling with depression and realized also that he would certainly have to leave Harvard, he was with Jean Vanier at L'Arche. One day, as Henri was working in the cramped archive there, he noticed a poster pinned on the door behind Simone Landrien's desk. She was responsible for organizing the archives at L'Arche, and she told him that the painting in the poster was by Rembrandt. She could see how engaged he was by it and told him he ought to buy a copy for himself. He was listening to her but couldn't take his eyes off the old man's hands and how they touch his son's shoulders. It was just a poster, but the image started churning something deep within him.

In 1986, still haunted by the image on the poster, Henri did something familiar by now: he went to see it for himself, as if the painting were another form of living human document, just like Thomas Merton or the fragile Anton Boisen he had visited decades earlier. He traveled to St. Petersburg to visit the palatial Hermitage Museum and made his way up the regal white marble, red-carpeted Grand Staircase to room 254, the Rembrandt Room, to see the painting itself.[7] There are twenty-two other Rembrandt paintings in this room, but Henri turned all of his attention to *The Prodigal Son.* He stood for hours staring at each brush stoke beneath the varnish and the way Rembrandt made the colors shift from luminous brightness to great stretches of ominous shadow on the large canvas. The museum guard thought that Henri was getting too close. Using sign language, since Henri's Russian and the guard's English were limited, they agreed on a compromise spot from which Henri could continue to examine the painting.

The painting and the parable differ in detail. In the Gospel of Luke, "The Parable of the Prodigal and His Brother" involves a wealthy father who divides his property between his two sons. The younger son goes traveling, spends all his money carelessly, and runs into trouble. There's a famine. He's penniless and needs work. The best job he can get is feeding pigs. He feels a twinge of remorse and decides to return to his father, apologize, and ask for a new kind of relationship with him. Before he reaches home, before he can even say anything, his father is giving him new clothes, has arranged to slaughter the fatted calf, and a party in his honor is about to begin. Enter the older brother. "Not so fast!" He confronts his father: "Your youngest son has broken all the rules that I've followed to the letter. He gets all the benefit while I'm still sweating from all the work I do." "Son," says his father, "you are always with me, and all that is mine is yours. But we had to celebrate and rejoice, because this brother of yours was dead and has come to life; he was lost and has been found" (Luke 15:31–32).

Rembrandt's painting is not a literal depiction of the parable. In his classic 1948 study of the life and work of Rembrandt, Jakob Rosenberg describes this monumental work, painted around 1688 or 1689, toward the end of Rembrandt's life:

> The father bends in frontal attitude over his kneeling son. Though his eyes are closed, his features glow with an august kindness. His hands, stiffened with old age, are broadly yet gently laid on the son's shoulders. The

prodigal has the appearance of a swineherd. His clothes and sandals are torn, his head is bald. With utter humility he presses his shadowed face against his father's breast. Of the attendant figures the old man on the right, standing erect and solemn, wears a dull red coat and a yellowish robe. Next to him, a little farther back, sits a bearded man with a broad black hat. Two others appear dimly in the background.… They look on silently and reflect the deep emotion of the main group.[8]

Rembrandt painted his interpretation of "the Christian idea of mercy with deepest solemnity, as though this were his spiritual testament to the world."[9] He elevated a recognizable human story about brothers, their father, and the actions and choices of each into something much bigger. "What is meant and represented here is the divine love and mercy in its power to transform Death into Life."[10]

Rembrandt Harmenszoon van Rijn, like Henri's other favorite artist, Vincent van Gogh, faced immense personal trials in the pursuit of his art. He was born in Leiden in 1606 and was not yet forty when a series of tragic events befell him. In 1640, his mother died. Two years later, his wife, Saskia van Uylenburgh, died after a long illness. They had four children together and only the youngest, Titus, survived beyond infancy. After Saskia died, Rembrandt hired a widow, Geertje Dirckx, to take care of young Titus. The relationship, whatever form it may have taken, resulted in Geertje launching a breach of promise claim that ended when she was confined to a mental hospital (or house of correction, depending on which biography you read). In 1649 Rembrandt hired a new housekeeper, Hendrickje Stoffels. She became his common-law wife and they had a child together. Meanwhile,

Rembrandt ran up debts, faced financial collapse several times, yet continued to paint to the end of his life. He died in Amsterdam in 1669.

The historian and Rembrandt expert Simon Schama says we should remember that Rembrandt was a nondenominational artist.

> Rembrandt came from a family in which the father was a Calvinist and the mother a practicing Catholic. At different times he himself was attracted to Remonstrants, Mennonites, and to highly unorthodox sects...whose emphasis on extreme scriptural simplicity appealed to a Christian for whom the Bible was an anthology of human drama. And he was able to paint and etch rabbis, predikants [Dutch Reformed ministers] and Mennonite lay preachers with equal conviction and sympathy.[11]

There in the Hermitage, as Henri looked, he began a deep decoding of the painting that was as personal as it was theological. He reflected on decades of his experiences of being the oldest of three brothers and on his difficult relationship with his father. In the resulting book that he wrote, Henri says he came to the realization that the painting had given him nothing less than "a context in which to discover that the final stage of the spiritual life is to so fully let go of all fear of the Father that it becomes possible to become like him...and to live out his divine compassion in my daily life."[12]

Henri said that he saw the entire Gospel in it, as well as the lives of all of his friends. He described it as "a mysterious window" that offered him a glimpse of the kingdom of God.[13] His longtime L'Arche colleague, Bill Clarke, SJ, says that when Henri looked through this "mysterious window" he also confronted his own woundedness:

When he speaks about the Prodigal Son and that whole beauty of the one coming home to the father, how you can articulate it, how he discovered himself as being the younger son and wanting to get away and running away and then gradually discovering how he's also the elder son, with his resentment and never being satisfied and working as a slave for the father rather than just being a beloved child. Then, finally, as he grew and became more at home with himself, to identify with the father in that story, and how the father has this great compassion, he began to think of his own gift of compassion and welcoming fatherhood. I don't think he ever became really at home in his own skin. He was always journeying toward that and articulating that journey for so many people—because it's everybody's journey.

The Return of the Prodigal Son is another element of Henri's creed. It is a personal testament of the faith that emerges from a lifetime of struggling with shadows. "People who have come to know the joy of God do not deny the darkness, but they choose not to live in it," he wrote toward the end of his book.[14] Henri also explained that it was the experience of discovering a sense of home in Daybreak that allowed him, finally, to address this darkness and feel able to move "from the kneeling, disheveled young son to the standing, bent-over old father, from the place of being blessed to the place of blessing."[15]

The book had already become a classic, confirming Henri Nouwen's reputation as one of the twentieth century's foremost writers of Christian spirituality. It was on the strength of the book's continuing success that Jan van den Bosch planned the documentary film. Henri had to prepare for this, even though he was physically exhausted. If you listen to some of the recordings that he made in these final years, you can hear a labored heaviness of breath. If you watch any of the late videos that were recorded, you can see his deeply lined and drained face. Yet, somehow, Henri still managed to animate himself with sweeping scooping gestures and make sure that the show would go on.

Toward the end of this especially difficult sabbatical break, difficult because there was never enough time to address everything that needed attention, Henri met Sue Mosteller in Toronto to discuss his eventual reentry into the world of Daybreak. He told her that he wanted to be there more, write more, and do more teaching.

> But right in the middle of that was his anxiety about all the things that were going on in his office and I remember saying to him, "Henri, if you go back to your office, you're dead. You can't do this! It's not gonna work because you get caught in all the daily stuff. It's the stuff you can't *not* be in." And he said, "I know, but I have to get reconnected. I can't just come home and not be rooted and connected."

It was a frustrating, inconclusive conversation after which Henri packed his bags for the trip to Holland to see his family and then fly on to Russia for the film shoot. He felt ready for that now. After all, he'd been reflecting deeply on this painting and the parable since his chance encounter a decade earlier. His 1992 book about it was selling well. And he had also been living his own version of it since 1932.

Henri's friend, the psychologist and theologian Robert Jonas, picks up the story from September 16 to September 21.

This was September 1996. Henri flew to his home country, Holland, and stayed at a hotel and he was going to meet his family before he went on. He then had a heart attack, in the hotel. I was told they couldn't get the gurney through the door so they actually lowered Henri down from the window. There's a kind of resonance with a Gospel story there.

On Monday, September 16, Henri was rushed from the hotel to the hospital in Hilversum, just east of Amsterdam. There, he learned that he had had a mild heart attack and was advised to cancel the Russian trip, but after their tests, was told he would likely be healthy enough to return to Canada quite soon.

"I talked to him by phone," continues Jonas. "I can't remember if I called him or he called me, but I said I was going to make arrangements to come to visit him in the hospital and Henri said, 'Don't come, Jonas, because they told me it's mild and I'll meet you in Toronto next week.'"

Others were less confident and began to make their way to Hilversum. Laurent Nouwen was at home when he received the news.

> I remember that when they phoned to tell me this, I asked what was the first plane I could take to Canada to see him and was told that I didn't need to worry as he was resting in a hospital practically around the corner, as it were. All the family gathered as quickly as possible and we could see he was going through a very difficult time, that he was struggling.

A large group of family and friends began to congregate in Hilversum. A priest heard Henri's confession, and gave him the anointing of the sick. He rallied and was well enough to be moved out of the intensive care unit. Amid their concerns for his well-being, Henri was worried about disrupting the Russian film shoot and all the complicated rescheduling that would now be required at the Hermitage Museum. He managed to take a few steps up and down the hospital corridor, walking very slowly. After a few days of keeping an all-night vigil, it seemed that Henri was going to pull through. All the signs looked good, and the family decided to shift from a constant vigil to visits during regular visiting hours. They were just minutes away, after all, should anything change in his condition.

"So, for the first time since his admittance, he spent the evening alone," says Laurent. Weakened by the first attack, although he seemed to have rallied, Henri could not survive the sudden catastrophic attacks that followed early in the morning of Saturday, September 21. Filled with sadness and remorse, Laurent adds, "He died with no one around him." Henri was sixty-four.

September 21, 1996, is a day she will never forget. Sue Mosteller, on the other side of the Atlantic, learned what had happened. Devastated, she retrieved Henri's will and in the file was another document. "I saw my name. I said, 'Oh that's nice. Henri left me something,' but didn't stop to read it." There would be funeral plans to attend to. Two, in fact. The first funeral was celebrated on September 25, 1996, in Utrecht Cathedral, with Cardinal Archbishop Simonis presiding. Jean Vanier gave the eulogy and Rodleigh Stevens, who had traveled to Utrecht to attend the funeral, was completely surprised by what he heard during the service.

I went to his funeral at the cathedral in Utrecht where he was ordained as a priest, and I met his family and friends and I saw another side of Henri's life which I didn't know anything about, and it sort of intrigued me to know how private Henri was when he was with us. We didn't know much about his private life until after he died. Then it became more evident to us how important we had become to him and what it was that he found in our friendship that he could draw inspiration from to write more in his books: the parallels that he found with our lives and his life and the spiritual world that he ministered in.

Henri's father understood that his son's home had become the Daybreak community in Canada and he proposed that Henri be buried there, rather than in the family plot in the Netherlands. Following his wishes, Laurent Nouwen made the arrangements and accompanied Henri's body to Canada. The box containing the coffin had a label: "The Human Remains of Henri Nouwen."

At Daybreak, Carolyn Whitney-Brown was busy in the carpentry shop—the Woodery. Henri had made it clear what he wanted well in advance. He said, "Keep me away from a funeral home, make a simple wooden coffin in our Woodery...bury me in a plot... where other members of Daybreak can also be buried...keep it very simple, very prayerful, and very joyful."[16]

"We had no experience of building caskets, so we built a broom closet, which we did know how to do. It was tall and slender and about right," explains Whitney-Brown. "We had some good advice from a local funeral home, good practical advice, like make the bottom of the broom closet stronger than you'd need to normally in a cabinet because you don't want the body to fall out the bottom. So there was a certain kind of humor as well as a practical quality."

As with any death, "the reality of it kind of comes and goes," she adds. Core members and assistants at Daybreak worked hard to complete the coffin in time. They were scrambling up to the very last minute. "The casket was ready and the lid was beautiful. We posed with the casket. We wrote messages to Henri on the back of the lid, where only he'd see them. And then I think it hit us that he actually wasn't going to see them. We kept thinking of how much he'd like this."

Robert Jonas was in Toronto with members of the Daybreak community to escort Henri's body from the airport chapel. "We opened the casket and there was Henri. Of course, that was shocking," he recalls.

> He was wearing a suit and we weren't used to seeing Henri in a suit and we felt that for this, his last appearance at Daybreak, he should be wearing his stoles. One of the women in the community and the person in charge of the chapel changed his suit to his robes and stole. Then we all drove in the hearse back to L'Arche Daybreak and there were days of mourning.

Henri's second funeral took place on September 28, at the nearest largest church in the vicinity of Daybreak: the Slovak Cathedral of the Transfiguration, a twenty minute drive away in Markham. It was crowded. "We began the funeral in Canada with how the one in Holland had ended," says Carolyn. "We welcomed his body with sunflowers. We surrounded it with just vases and vases of sunflowers."

Sue Mosteller saw the funeral as a demonstration of Henri's radical transformation of the Daybreak community and how he had encouraged them to mark any death in the community. "He always said it was to celebrate the person, to really allow the person to shine, to tell stories, to weep, to laugh, and to have all the human emotions around the fact that this was somebody who was very deeply loved and who belonged. This was the essence of everything he taught us."

Michelle O'Rourke has been deeply influenced by Henri's emphasis on being ready for death. She uses this theme in her palliative care work today, building on her research into Henri's spirituality of death and how he emphasized the importance of actually preparing for it. Her influential book on palliative care is based on Henri's ideas. "His belief was that all of us need to reflect on and befriend our death whether we are facing a life-threatening illness or not."[17]

Sue Mosteller noted how Henri's Canadian funeral brought many disparate worlds and interests together into that crowded church: politicians, peace activists, church hierarchy, members of the military and the police, creative types (including Fred Rogers, the Mr. Rogers of children's television fame), journalists, curious locals, friends, and hundreds of people from all walks of life who knew Henri through his books. "We had this marvelous celebration. People came from far and wide," she says.

Jonas performed a lamentation on the shakuhachi flute.

It was liturgy, says Mosteller. "The communion was wonderful— a spectacular coming together, everybody was invited to come forward, either to receive communion or receive a blessing. And everyone came forward."

And it was also theater. "We have a troupe, The Spirit Movers. They are a dance troupe, in wheelchairs, and the people with disabilities and the assistants, they all danced up the aisle with the offertory procession, with flowers and the gifts to be put on the altar. Amazing? Amazing! It was an incredible celebration!"

Then there was the burial. "The burial too was very beautiful," says Carolyn.

We threw shovels of earth and spoke about Henri by the graveside and talked about memories of Henri at other funerals, and the kinds of things he'd said. The sadness was huge and the shock was huge. Being able to throw a giant liturgical celebration in the style of Henri without Henri leading it felt bittersweet. It felt like we were doing the things that we knew how to do so well because Henri had done that kind of big, joyful, liturgical event with so much energy and joy that we knew how to build the feeling and how to make it happen. But to do it because of Henri's death, rather than to welcome him home alive was really hard.

When Sue Mosteller returned to her office, she had to consider the meaning of that document from Henri with her name on it. The day after Robert Ellsberg returned to his office at Orbis Books, he received a letter. It was from Henri.

The Wounded Healer

*"I just join the legions of others who have been
transformed by his writing."*

For many in Henri's immediate circle, the most important question after the funeral was: What do we do now?

When Robert Jonas returned to his retreat center, the Empty Bell, he reflected on twenty years of intense friendship with Henri. He says he "began to think about the Gospel story when Jesus died and the disciples were wondering: 'This is the end of the world. What are we going to do now, with the Master gone?'"

What eventually emerged within the membership of that first Nouwen circle was a sense of responsibility to ensure that what Henri had written and spoken about would continue to be heard. "We have to bring the message ourselves. Henri's basic message of belovedness, that we are all 'the beloved,' like Jesus," concluded Jonas. "Something happened in us where *we* had to claim his message more deeply because *he* wasn't saying it anymore."

Sue Mosteller learned from the document with her name on it that Henri had asked her to become his literary executrix—that meant taking responsibility for managing his publishing rights and permissions. As she quickly discovered, even dead authors have contracts that need negotiating. She managed all the rights issues for Henri's books that were still in the works, plus the rights to everything else written by Henri during his lifetime. "So that was the beginning of that journey: a very beautiful gift, but also a difficult gift, because it was a learning curve that went straight up in the air for me."[1]

Robert Ellsberg said he returned to his office at Orbis Books, feeling numb. "It just seemed impossible to think, 'Well, that's the end of that friendship, that story, that collaboration.' Twenty years!" He was thankful that just a few weeks earlier, he had been able to send Henri the special plaque he had commissioned to celebrate the success of the book they had worked on together, *With Burning Hearts.* On his second day at work after returning from Canada, he writes,

> The mail arrives and there's a letter from Henri, his unmistakable hand. He'd written it about ten days before he died. It was very typical Henri. He said, "Boy oh boy! Thank you for this plaque. I don't know where I have a place grand enough to display it!" He recalled this wonderful evening we'd had, how much he looked forward to working together in the years to come, and it was the first realization that I had that this friendship was not over. In the next ten years, I published many books by and about Henri, and he's continued to be an even more important figure in my life—even more, I think, than he was in all those years before.

Adam: God's Beloved and *Bread for the Journey: A Daybook of Wisdom and Faith* were published in 1997. *Sabbatical Journey: The Diary of His Final Year* appeared in 1998. Since then Henri has been much excerpted and anthologized. Mosteller began the discussion about what to do with all the manuscripts, papers, clippings, notes, financial files, phone bills, letters, and photographs that Henri had kept in various places throughout his nomadic career. The collection was both huge and scattered. Some of it was with the Nouwen family in the Netherlands, some of it in archive at Yale University, and much of it was in the more than a hundred storage boxes that he had filled during his decade at Daybreak. The objective was to gather all of this material into a single archive, preferably not too far from Daybreak. Once assembled, this messy mass of materials could be organized according to professional archival standards. Location negotiations began with the University of St. Michael's College in the University of Toronto, and deaccessioning negotiations with archivists at Yale. They all agreed and on September 21, 2000, the fourth anniversary of Henri's death, the university's John M. Kelly Library opened the doors of the Henri J.M. Nouwen Archives to students, researchers, scholars, and anyone else interested in getting to know more about him.

Gabrielle Earnshaw's formal title is head of St. Michael's Archival and Manuscript Collections and Archivist of the Henri J.M. Nouwen Archives and Research Collection. "We have almost everything Henri Nouwen wrote in his lifetime in these archives," she explains, "as well as all the records that he would have been accumulating in his life as a writer, in his life as a priest, in his life as a teacher, as a speaker, as a retreat leader. All of the records would be here."

Sometimes, a job is just another contract, and on rare occasions it emerges as a life-changing experience. "I didn't know him when I first started working here," she adds.

> I was attracted to the job ad because it said L'Arche, and I had heard of Jean Vanier. I thought, well, if there's some-body who lived at L'Arche Daybreak I might be interested in doing their archival records. As an archivist you usually go from one person's record to another and you're expected to maintain some kind of objectivity. Well, I

don't think I have distance from my subject! I have been personally, and I don't think it would be too strong a word to say: transformed, by Henri Nouwen's writing.

Although she never met Henri, through her close reading of his entire archival collection she has formed a uniquely powerful portrait.

I find Henri Nouwen lived his life with great authenticity, with great integrity, and he had as many problems as the rest of us. He was not free from great anxiety, huge bouts of alienation and feeling lonely, and yet he was able to write about it and then offer it as a witness. He used the life of Jesus this way. He used the life of Thomas Merton this way. He used the life of ordinary people in this way. When he saw the trapeze artists that he became so influenced by and so interested in, in 1991, and for the rest of his life, he saw in this act a wonderful metaphor for the spiritual life. There is the flyer reaching out, the catcher catches him. That could have been fodder enough for a book, but that isn't all he wanted to write about. He wanted to know who these people were and he did his own intensive research on them. He joined them in a caravan, did interviews with them. We have a 300-page document of oral history interviews that he did with these artists. He is not only one of the most non-mechanical people I know, but he learned how to rig a net for the trapeze because it was important for him to know what these individuals were up against when they were performing their wonderful act. He had to know how you rig these swings, these trapezes.

I think that it is his very life that has been most transformative for me. His books! Every time I read one or pick it up for a researcher because they've asked me about it, I find it never fails to address something I'm questioning in my own life. So it's very personal, and I just join the legions of others who have been transformed by his writing.

Jean Vanier celebrates Henri's giftedness as a writer. "First of all, he understood L'Arche, as he showed especially in the book *Adam: God's Beloved.* Also, he had what I call the sacrament of the word. He knew how to say things that people would listen to and had a power of the word, especially the written word. And third, he was extremely authentic. He would have lost himself if he had stayed at Harvard or Yale, but he found himself at L'Arche. He helped people to find themselves, to discover a vision. You can see that his vision continues to touch me and flows through my letters even after his death in 1996."[2]

Robert Ellsberg explains the often surprising difference between encountering Henri in print and in person:

> His impact has been felt by countless people who never knew him in person. I think that for a lot of his following, people who went and heard him speak, he was a fantastically charismatic speaker, retreat leader, conference speaker, and he had this inimitable way of speaking. It was almost acting out on stage what he was talking about. People responded to that. Even when he was alive, when I thought of Henri I thought of that person, the person who made such an impact when you met him personally. His books didn't register with me that much, but I began to appreciate his genius at being able to express things in their simplicity, in their essence, and the fact that this came out of not only deep learning and scholarship, but out of a restless practice and effort to live out what he was

writing about. I think the books achieved more and more depth and authenticity as he lived that out more authentically in his last ten years. I think that one of the things that Henri really did for me was to make me more aware of the Christian journey as a kind of meeting place with Jesus in one's life, and to understand one's own story and one's own journey in relation to the story of Jesus.

Working with Henri was a defining life experience, as well as a blessing, for Nathan Ball:

> First of all, he had a deep and very articulate way of telling me that my life was important and that in spite of various options I could explore in terms of how I want to live my life, that I should and could be very faithful to my heart's deepest longing. I began to realize that this had to do with living with people with disabilities and in a community. Henri helped me to realize that L'Arche could be very transformational in society. He believed in my life in a very father-like way. I got a blessing—many people don't get a blessing from their own father. I got a blessing from a couple of fathers, and Henri was one of them. I've been deeply blessed by two men in my life: the first was my father. I struggled with my relationship with my father and I wanted an affirmation and a blessing from him. That took longer to come than I had wanted. With Henri, the blessing probably came sooner than I wanted, and because of its intensity, it took me a while to receive it, to listen to it, and finally accept it. As my relationship with my own father evolved and as with my relationship with Henri, I realized that I am truly blessed to have had these two blessings. They are really important anchors in my life.

Fr. Robert Beloin followed in Henri's footsteps to Yale. He was ordained in 1973, and after teaching at the University of Louvain for five years, he returned to the United States for a decade of parish life in New Haven. He was named chaplain at the St. Thomas More Center at Yale University in 1994. Father Bob, as he is known to his community, identifies Henri as one of the most important influences in his spiritual development as a Catholic priest.

> I think he brought a freshness to appreciating the Christian life and the insights of the Christian faith beyond abstract dogmas and stale language that was tired, and really could not carry the mystery very well anymore. I think Henri had a genius for finding mystery within the language, to unpack great ideas and really made the Christian faith dynamic, interesting, and accessible for people. If you think of concentric circles, he didn't live on the edge and the periphery of what you could talk about. He talked about the core things: reconciliation, healing, acceptance. All of that stuff is at the core of Christian experience, the core of Christian spirituality that we can sometime forget. He was very life-giving and life-affirming. People walked away from him, I think, feeling better about themselves and better about life and its meaning, its cohesiveness. It made sense. Nouwen didn't get bogged down in institutional questions. He didn't write about the ordination of women or birth control or the kind of hot-button topics that could get you kind of aligned, in the institutional sense, on the left or right. He avoided that kind of stuff and stayed to what was important to spirituality. That is his great contribution to the church.

Meanwhile, at Yale Divinity School, Henri's former students there chose to remember him by paying for the conversion of the small Byzantine chapel on the lower level of the Yale Divinity Library. In 2007, the circular chapel was rededicated as the Nouwen Chapel with a central triptych painted to reflect Native American spirituality by John Giuliani, a Connecticut Jesuit and icon artist. Giuliani's center panel depicts Christ, and the outer panels portray Henri surrounded by some of the people who especially influenced him, including Blessed Oscar Romero, Martin Luther King Jr., Vincent van Gogh, Thomas Merton, and Adam Arnett. Off to the side of the chapel there's a tiny pipe organ.

Posthumous friendships are difficult, and like all friendships, they are subject to tidal variations, rising and falling with sometimes unpredictable intensity. They are often tinged with regret about opportunities missed, inexplicable gaps, strange silences, and sudden unaccountable breaks. Peter Naus recalls a memorable conversation with Henri:

> I will not forget this because it was a few months, as it turned out, before his death. I called him when I knew I would be retiring in September, 1996. I had felt increasingly disappointed with the fact that we had lost contact, I thought. So I called him, and we agreed that we would reconnect and that there would be much more opportunity for me because I would not have any more work commitments. We said that we would meet in the fall. But, of course, he died.

Henri's diaries published after his death revealed troubling details to Naus and to many others who thought they knew him.

> I took responsibility and felt guilty for having lost touch somewhat with Henri when I read his diary—his last

diary. When I went through this book, I felt so badly. I thought that it was a tortured kind of self-reflection. Maybe I could not have a done a whole lot, but he really needed friends and I felt badly. Of course, he died before we could reconnect and I also had to deal with that. What helped me is that as I was doing interviews in Holland about friendships with Henri, several of his friends, without being in any way prodded by me, spontaneously said that in the last several years, and still I don't know why, but they didn't have much contact. There's something else here and I don't know what it is, but there was a certain withdrawing on Henri's part, especially from his earlier friends. I don't know why that would have been, but I do think this could be an important piece to think about.

That may be speculative, but Peter's explanation of Henri's central message is definitive:

In purely psychological terms, translated, the core theme of his writing is: Am I lovable? Am I valuable? Am I worthwhile? Spiritually interpreted, for Henri, that was: God has declared that you *are*, because you are "My Beloved." Henri's spiritual insight was that we can only ever come to grips with the psychological question of our own value if we can believe, and hopefully experience, that there is a "prior love," as he calls it, which is that God loves us. God's love means it doesn't matter what you do, whether you do something that is good or something that is bad, something that is valuable or something that is not valuable. "You are lovable in My eyes."

Robert Ellsberg identifies the central theme in Henri's work as Christian life seen "as an encounter with Jesus, among our neighbors, in response to the needs of our time." Nouwen presents readers with "a challenge to escape from the compulsiveness of our culture, to find a resting place, to find a place of peace, and to become a source of peace for others." What makes this so compelling for Ellsberg is that this message came from "such a complicated person, not some kind of plaster-cast of healthy mindedness, but somebody approachable and somebody that we can all identify with."

This "complicated" Henri, although essentially an autobiographical writer, chose to be open only about certain selective aspects of his life. He remained circumspect, if not silent, publically at least, about other issues. In 1994, Henri wrote, enigmatically, "all my life I harbored a strange curiosity for the disobedient life that I myself didn't dare to live, but which I saw being lived by many around me."[3]

Naus identifies the source of Henri's cautiousness about disclosure this way:

> Henri had an aversion to any kind of scandal, particularly scandal in the church. He was a very faithful servant and was afraid of being engaged in anything that would cause scandal. He had very much identified with what I perceive was in the Catholic Church, this aversion of scandal of any kind. I think he bought into that, and he had for a long time.

Richard Sipe remembers challenging Henri about his resistance to confronting Church teaching publically:

> Henri couldn't do that. He would pray around that, and he would preach around that, and he would find scripture

around that, but he couldn't say, "Look, your teaching, your discipline on this is wrong." Now, he was in a very difficult position because if he said that, what would that mean for his personal life? It was too close to home for him, too close to that little unfinished business in his life, which he handled in his own way, and in a beautiful way.

His brother, Laurent, agrees, and says this is because Henri did not want to "disappoint the world" by bringing attention to what he considered to be personal rather than Church issues. "Henri had been deeply affected by that internal struggle, a thorn in his flesh, that had been very painful. But, on the other hand, it would not have been the solution for him to be more open about it." Henri was not looking for solutions. Rather he was asking, "How can I live and how can I be accepted, even with the pain I live in my heart?"

Ronald Rolheiser portrays Henri as "radically honest" and "a saint in progress." In the book he dedicated to Henri, he calls him "our generation's Kierkegaard" and "perhaps the best spiritual writer of our generation."[4] Henri's true gift as a writer, Rolheiser says, is that he manages to integrate three important qualities in his writing: it is faith-filled but nondenominational, it is art not politics, and it is highly crafted simplicity. The books are faith-filled because of the way he made them

confessional without being denominational. It catches people by surprise. He doesn't write as some secular analyst, and he doesn't hide the fact that he's a priest, a Roman Catholic priest. That's not the voice he uses. It's always Henri. In fact, very few people call him Father Nouwen. He's Henri, and Henri is speaking as a human being. In that sense, he's deeply theistic, and Christian, and committed, and he even speaks from a clear denominational stance, but that is not what you hear.

Henri writes as an artist, not as a politician of religion. "By and large, artists like doing art. They are really clear: 'I do art.' It's not that they are unaware or disinterested, it's just not what they do."

As for simplicity in his writing:

> Henri used to write his books lots of times over to try to get them more simple, to rid them of their complexity without, at the same time, making them simplistic, so that his books speak to the heart. They speak at a certain depth and so precisely because he worked at this consciously to try and eliminate the technical terms. Where he could use a smaller word, he'd use a smaller word. Again, that was part of his genius. In fact, it's all of his major books, but probably nowhere more true than in that great book he wrote at the end, *The Return of the Prodigal Son*. It's a masterpiece, and that book is utterly simple *and* really deep. Nobody is going to say it's a simplistic book, but you don't have to know any technical theology. You don't have to know any biblical scholars, and there are no footnotes. It's simply his insight.

When Henri died, many people lost a friend and mentor. Laurent lost a brother, his older brother who lived on the other side of the Atlantic for more than half of his life. After Henri's death, Laurent felt that he might have neglected his older brother, "Or at least, I didn't give him the attention, the kind of brotherhood he was looking for." He says his sister and brothers "had a good relationship with Henri, but I have my personal doubts it was sufficient, what we gave him. But on the other hand, I have to say, Henri did ask sometimes too much." But when Henri died, any "limitations which we had as brothers, from both sides" simply fell away.

It changed my life completely and I am very grateful that he was my brother. Henri is a great inspiration, an ongoing inspiration and I can only be grateful for that. What I learned from Henri is that inclusiveness of the weak is the essence of becoming human. This is an important awareness because placing people who are poor, weak, or disabled, in the center of our community, in the center of our life, if we can't do that, then we lose all our humanity. Henri gave me that vision that inspires me today, every moment of the day.

In November 2010, Laurent had one more brotherly duty to perform. Just as there had been two funerals for Henri there would also be two burials. The Sacred Heart Cemetery in Richmond Hill had run out of space, meaning that others who had died in the Daybreak community would now have to be buried in Richmond Hill's Anglican cemetery. In order to respect Henri's wishes to be buried among them, a second burial service was held on a chilly November day at St. John's Anglican Cemetery, where the team at the Woodery had restored an old wooden bench for visitors to the new Daybreak community's plot.[5]

The man who in 1995 wrote, "When I was close to death, I experienced one thing: I didn't want to be alone.... Dying is maybe not even the great agony; it is dying alone,"[6] was, finally, no longer alone.

WHERE BIOGRAPHY AND AUTOBIOGRAPHY INTERSECT

"...that unfinished piece of business..."

Early in 2008, I was at my desk in Ottawa when the phone rang. It was Michael W. Higgins. He asked if I would work with him on a biographical documentary for CBC Radio on the life and legacy of Henri Nouwen. Our previous collaboration was on a documentary about how saints are formally recognized in the Catholic Church.[1] It was time for a new kind of project, he said. Within weeks I was in Amsterdam, microphone in hand, digital recording device safely in my shoulder-bag, walking across the cobblestones of Dam Square in front of the Koninklijk Paleis. This large classical stone building dates back to 1655, the Dutch Golden Age. It began life as Amsterdam's city hall, and then, in 1813, it was renovated and expanded to become a palace for the Dutch royal family.

As I walked around this large open square, I recorded some of the sounds you need for a radio documentary—passing trams and passersby, the bass rumble of a plane high overhead, an angry dog on the other side of the square, young women in a tight cluster whispering to each other then bursting into laughter, the sudden tinny blare of a drum-based ringtone on a cell phone and the silent fumble to make it stop, endless bicycle bells each sounding a slightly different note, and then a great resonant church bell off in the distance, announcing it was finally time for the first interview, about one of our friends, the dead.

The interviews had a shadow over them. In *Our Second Birth*, published two years after his death, Henri sounded the warning: "The idea of people posthumously exploring the details of my personal life frightens me, but I am reassured by the knowledge of having friends who know me intimately and will guard me not only in life, but also in memory."[2]

Biographers prefer that such guardians wait outside the room until some of the preliminary work is over. Readers and listeners want to know what really happened, what didn't happen, what could have happened, and all the whys and why-nots in between. Reading a biography, we compare and contrast someone else's life challenges and choices with our own in a delicate dance with those partners: biography and autobiography. As we read, sometimes leading and sometimes following, we continue that ancient Biblical tradition that calls on each of us to consider the lives of all those people of faith who came before us. We are challenged to consider how people, then, strove to experience life as a beloved child of God and how we, today, might do the same. It is possible, as Abraham Joshua Heschel asserted, to summarize the Bible in just one word: "Remember."[3]

And remember we do. We read about them in biographies and we talk about them in our conversations with the living. We remember the saints, the sinners, the confident, the lost, the blessed, the confused, the dangerous. We remember all those fellow pilgrims on a journey whose ultimate destination lies far beyond the Plaza del Obradoiro outside the Cathedral of Santiago de Compostela, or the Piazza Inferiore outside the Basilica of Saint Francis in Assisi. We remember through the centuries. And we remember across geographical distances that we only sometimes get to travel.

I remember being mystified by all the languages I heard as a child, the mumbled Latin and the rarely amplified (in those days) English. I wondered why Sunday missals in England seemed always to be printed in Belgium, where I knew neither Latin nor English were the local languages. Those foreign printers must have been really smart, working in all those different languages at once, I thought. As I put another holy card between its flimsy red-edged pages, my missal grew thicker each year. The binding finally gave way, and the book with its frayed ribbon markers disappeared long ago. I can't remember when, but I do remember those cards. Soft-focused pastel portraits, some with gold and serrated edges. St. Anthony holding the Baby Jesus in one hand and a perfectly arced white lily in the other. A fragile St. Francis, eyes to the sky, surrounded by a well-behaved family of birds. Barefooted and robes flowing, Jesus cradles a seemingly freshly laundered woolly lamb. Closer to home, St. Werburgh holds a miniature version of the church dedicated to her in one hand, a crozier in the other, and at her feet a symbol of one of her miracles: geese.[4] Even as a child, I knew that I was being encouraged to consider something about *me* as I looked at these card reminders of *them*. Later, when Thomas Merton entered my life, I became more aware of the complexity of what I was really being asked to accomplish. "The problem of sanctity and salvation is in fact the problem of finding out who I am and of discovering my true self."[5]

The Christian tradition encourages us to seek out models of holiness and inspiration wherever and however we might find them. This is a long-standing invitation and it is wonderfully anarchic. We can after all pick any story we wish, not just the official ones—sometimes not even real ones—and compare them with our own. Despite the painstaking efforts of the gatekeepers of that elite club of the canonized, we seekers and believers around the world have always made it clear who our authentic saints are. Robert Ellsberg says it was through working alongside Dorothy Day on the *Catholic Worker* newspaper that he "learned to know and love the saints—not just legendary figures from Christian history but as friends and contemporaries, as members of the family, which is how she talked about them."[6] Consequently, not all saints are dead, neither are they always churchgoing.

I like to think of us, each carrying around a set of blank cards and we can add details to them in any way we choose. Henri Nouwen's card isn't blank, though, and two decades after his death, the questions of legacy become even more important. His vocation and mission illustrate his commitment to and pursuit of spiritual integration. He spoke and wrote personally about this for four decades in the second half of the twentieth century, encouraging those who read his work to consider themselves as the beloved children of God. He held in balance two perspectives which I believe are defining narratives of the century he lived through and the one we are now in: spirituality as quest and psychology as insight. Michelle O'Rourke calls this Henri's "unique way of bridging the spiritual and secular worlds."[7] By wrapping each in the other, he extended the reach of both.

When I began to look at Henri, I had none of this knowledge. It began to take shape interview by interview as, microphone in hand, I listened to people describe their Henri. Some were the protective guardians he had hoped for, like the one who said in an early interview, "I am very aware of the fact that there is a thin line, as it were, between being a friend and being a confidant. I don't want to cross that line and if I get to be a little cautious, that's why it is." Others had so much to say that we often needed to extend our studio time.

The documentary about Henri aired in a series called *Ideas*, and I am intrigued by Jean Vanier's explanation of the source of ideas. He says they "come from a world turned upside down."[8] From his perspective as a broadcaster, Bernie Lucht, the series coproducer, is interested in what ideas *do*.

> They shape how we think and speak about the world, how we behave, how we see ourselves, individually, and in society. Ideas drive imagination; they determine how we conceive the past, the present and the future; they inform our political and social arrangements, our arts and culture, science, technology and religion, our personal relationships and beliefs.[9]

These words filtered the interviews and the search through Nouwen's books, forty of them still in print, available in thirty languages, and untold millions sold. This certainly is a man of influence.

In a documentary, you work with what you get, and between his carefully nuanced books and the interviews, we had Henri fragments with fraying edges to work with. All the little pieces of Henri when combined still comprised only a limited perspective. As his brother says, "I see the way we look at Henri today, and a lot of people who read his books today that do not know him from a personal side. They create another person, generally a very nice person, a very wise person. They do not realize that he paid dearly for what he wrote."

Nice or wise, most lives are only ever recalled through fragments rather than extended lines of elegantly clear narrative. How much easier it would have been to create a novel Henri. "In the shadow of the Second World War, a young couple struggle to do the best for their young family. Their oldest son makes a choice that means that there will be no grandchildren from him. They thank God they have three other children. He chooses to serve God and leaves them behind to live in another country where, one day…" This Henri novel could even have an endorsement on the back cover from Thomas Merton, who would advise readers to buy it because it was about being "called to share with God the work of *creating* the truth of our identity,"[10] and certainly worth the price on the cover.

Henri invites his readers to do their own identity work in fact, not fiction. Each of us will likely have our own Henri where biography (his story) intersects with autobiography (yours and mine). It's what we do with these fragments and stories that counts. Back then to the beginning and those words of the novelist George Eliot. In the final pages of *Middlemarch*, she presents the case that our lives are constantly touched by the example of others, real or imagined, and their actions, large and—especially—small. "For there is no creature whose inward being is so strong that it is not greatly determined by what lies outside it." Influence often comes through those small, almost imperceptible details whose effects are both lasting and "incalculably diffusive, for the growing good of the world is partly dependent on unhistoric acts."[11]

In this book, I have lifted a few of Henri's biographical cobblestones, not to throw them at anyone, but to reveal some of the autobiographical sand that lies underneath. I also encourage you to do the same. I conclude with an explanation of nine points of contact that I discovered with Henri, places where biography touches autobiography. Before I begin, though, there's a simple intersecting detail that I choose not to count in that set of nine. Henri and I share the same birthday, January 24, the feast of St. Francis de Sales, patron saint of writers, journalists, and the Catholic press. Henri died at sixty-four, which is my age as I write this, making this one small place where I hope biography and autobiography actually part company.

Here, then, are nine things I discovered buried in that sand.

ONE: BE OPEN TO BLESSING

Like Henri, I left my family and friends in one country to live and work in another. I left England in 1974 when I was twenty-two, and I returned infrequently. The people I knew and loved gradually began to slip into archetype and myth. This made any visit home fraught with unrealistic expectations for great meaningful revelations or significant new beginnings. Sometimes a drive in the country with your parents is just that—a chance to feed the ducks before a nice cup of tea.

My father and my mother are dead now. Unlike Henri, I never felt compelled to ask them if they loved me. In the year 2000, I discovered how well my father knew me, though. He left school at the age of fifteen, became an apprentice, then fought in the Second World War and when he returned he never—ever—spoke about any of his experiences in it. As in many British households during the 1950s and 1960s, the war and things German were topics of nonconversation. When I took a job with a Catholic publishing house that summer, it came with the requirement to attend the Frankfurt Book Fair in Germany each October. That was the summer my dad's health began to fail. In August, just three weeks before he died, my mother telephoned to tell me, "Your dad wants you to know that it's all right with him for you to go to that book fair, you know." A blessing of sorts.

TWO: BE OPEN TO THE MOMENT

In one of her vivid interviews about Henri, Carolyn Whitney-Brown presents the brilliant image of Henri's two books: "One is the book that Henri wrote forty times, yet couldn't quite live; the other is the book that Henri lived for almost sixty-five years, yet couldn't quite write."[12] Whether or not anyone considers themselves to be an author, I am certainly challenged by this image of a life as a book where intention and experience are not always aligned. The first book is the one we inhabit. As life circumstances change, so new chapters evolve. Then there's that other book, the book of reflection. That's the book with all those pages waiting to be filled if only we stop for a moment to look around and start to notice. The chaotic and constantly interrupted rush of daily and increasingly digital life so easily diverts us from this. Maybe you've seen Thornton Wilder's play *Our Town*. In a final touching scene, young Emily, now dead, is brought back to life as an invisible observer of her family one ordinary morning. "It goes so fast. We don't have time to look at one another.... I didn't realize. So all that was going on and we never noticed."[13] I can take the time to look if I choose.

Three: Be open to friends

I understand loyalty anew after speaking to friends and colleagues of Henri Nouwen. Such powerful bonds. His letters, phone bills, and travel costs reveal how much he thrived on maintaining his relationship with them in return. It was a lifetime of hard work. Henri's example made me think of my friendships that span three time zones, as it were. I think of all my old friends who bookend the past, my here and now friends, and no less important, the new friendships, unknown to me now, that will populate the rest of my life. Friendship is about more than nostalgia; it requires being open to newness. It's also about not being naïve. Wherever there is friendship, because of the things we do and especially the things we don't do, or the things we do say and the things we don't say, the need for forgiveness is always closer than we ever realize. In

"Realism," one of the essays in *The Givenness of Things*, the wise Marilynne Robinson writes,

> We know how deeply we can injure one another by denying forgiveness. We know how profoundly we can impoverish ourselves by failing to find value in one another. We know that respect is a profound alleviation, which we can offer and too often withhold.... A theology of grace is a higher realism, an ethics of truth. Writers know this.[14]

Writers may continue to encourage me along the way with their ideas about friendship, but it's up to me to do my own relationship work.

Four: Be guided

There's a wonderful web of deep connections in Henri's life story that extends over great stretches of time. He actively sought out and met individuals who could help him. Each of them extended out into yet another community of connections: Cardinal Alfrink, Gordon Allport, Anton Boisen, Thomas Merton, John Eudes Bamberger, John Vesey, Gustavo Gutiérrez, Jean Vanier, Rodleigh Stevens, to name only nine on Henri's extensive list. This was not the pursuit of selfie photo ops with celebrities, but the recognition that he wanted the guidance of a broad community of experience and wisdom.

Henri also discovered nurturing mentors in people he could never meet, especially Vincent van Gogh and Rembrandt. This reminds me to remember the past and to not fall into the trap of seeing wisdom as belonging to my generation only. A good mentor can be virtual, someone I can bring back from the past to influence my ideas about the present moment. As my career shifted focus from theater, to education, to broadcasting, to publishing, and eventually writing, I value the communities of mentors, those generous and often really tough souls who, dead or alive, have helped me along the way. I have a list and there's more room on the page.

Five: Be useful

I used to laugh at the detail in Henri's life that in his later years he ran off with the circus. It sounds like the punch line to a questionable joke, until you know what he was really doing: addressing unfinished business from his past that was initiated by a surprise encounter in the present. Like Henri the journalist, intent on finding out what really made things tick, I feel a sense of responsibility to keep looking and learning about more than just me. I like the words that St. Bernard of Clairvaux uses about what we do with what we learn. There are some who

> long to know for the sole purpose of knowing, and that is shameful curiosity; others who long to know in order to become known, and that is shameful vanity.... There are others still who long for knowledge to sell its fruits for money or honors, and this is shameful profiteering; others again who long to know in order to be of service, and this is charity. Finally, there are those who long to know in order to benefit themselves, and this is prudence.[15]

I find in Henri a compelling example of lifelong learning, and in St. Bernard sound advice to ensure that this approach to learning is balanced between being of service to others and being beneficial to my own development.

Six: Be patient

He may have had a clear sense of his path when he was six, but he spent the next fifty-eight years becoming the Henri he was discovering himself to be as he went about trying to accomplish that task. Along the way, he uncovered many layers of unfinished business. To me, this is the single-most moving aspect of Henri's life, his example of holding things in suspension that he could not resolve. Rather than seeing problems as things he needed to fix, these became conditions and circumstances for him to experience. Needing to attend to unfinished business is, in Richard Sipe's words, "that universal struggle." It's also what Robert Frost immortalized as those two roads "diverged in a wood" and that made him sorry he "could not travel both."[16]

For Henri, as for me, this kind of discernment requires patience and hard work. As Richard Sipe cautions, some important insights only surface in midlife and later. "But isn't that the way with creative people, that their development oftentimes is slower, but it's deeper and their constructions, their thoughts, their insights, they become powerful for all sorts of people because they hit that universal struggle. And I think that's what Henri did. Out of his deprivation was his creativity."

I'll try to not stop looking. Or in those words that doctors use so benignly, consider the practice of mindfulness and an approach of "watchful waiting."

SEVEN: BE AWARE OF YOUR ROLE

Radio is a fleeting medium. I often describe it as tap water, running somewhere in the background until it makes an irritating drip and is turned off. It can be the same with writing. You never know where it ends up or what it does when it gets there. The Canadian poet and Catholic priest, Pier Giorgio di Cicco, writes:

> Sometimes you create because it is
> just the thing to do, and what you create is
> inadvertent, like a house for birds,
> or like guests who come not knowing

bail a man out of loneliness; sometimes a poem
will come that has no joy and it will go to someone
like a divinizing.[17]

On rare occasions, you do get to find out. In 2015, CBC Radio invited listeners to identify programs that had had a powerful impact on their lives. David Hagel had something he wanted to share. Late one night, he was driving his tractor, gathering hay for baling on his cattle and grain farm in Cabri. That sounds as if it should be in Italy, but it's deep in Canada's agricultural heartland in southwest Saskatchewan. His wife and farming partner of twenty years, Leone, had died of cancer a few months earlier, and he wasn't sure he wanted this way of life anymore.

> It's late at night. I'm about a mile away from home. I catch a glimpse of the stars. I can't remember if there was a moon, but I'm kind of lost in my own thoughts and feeling a little bad about the job I'm doing because it didn't feel right. I turned the radio on. It didn't matter what I was listening to. I was hearing a program on Henri Nouwen. Probably what perked my interest was some advice he gave to a friend of his who had lost a child. Henri was able to communicate to them through his own experience and the experience of his faith that every life matters, that even God grieves when someone dies. No amount of wishing and hoping can change the fact that we don't have them with us physically, but they are with us in a profound way, emotionally and spiritually. What Henri Nouwen taught me and what I gained from that one night in the tractor was that each life makes a difference. All we have to do is let go of fear and choose to be unselfish.[18]

After I heard that, I had to track him down. David Hagel is in his midfifties now and halfway through a training program that will see him ordained as a deacon in the archdiocese of Regina in Saskatchewan in 2018. Hearing Henri by chance that night in his tractor turned things around. In our conversation he told me, "It was like baling all night and welcoming the sunrise to know that all that other stuff was behind me now. It was a new morning and after that I started to feel better."

I asked if anything changed on the farm after Leone died.

> I know for animals it's based on instinct, but it didn't take them very long to recognize that it was just me now. Leone had ways with animals, especially certain cows in our herd that almost felt like friends to her. She could provide that calming influence. She always told me that I yelled too much when I was with the cows. The attitude in the animals around the farm changed. It felt like they too were confused. I had to find new creative ways to get things done. Yes, there was a shift in our relationship— meaning me and my animals! I'm a lot calmer with them. I like to think that's part of Leone's spirit in part of what I do.

This reminds me to remember my specific role. Henri is the messenger, not me. I don't want to mess it up by getting in the way.

EIGHT: BE UNFILTERED

Henri's example of seeing right through to the heart of a person is an enormous challenge in this age of ability. As with Henri, it took a visit to a L'Arche community for me to begin to understand this. The simplicity of this tiny incident is what gave it such power. I was at the main community of L'Arche in Trosly-Breuil, working with Jean Vanier on the final edits for his 2004 book on the Gospel of St. John.[19] We worked together, uninterrupted, in his tiny cottage from 9:00 AM until noon for five days. For the rest of the time I simply observed the community at work. On the first evening I joined the largest *foyer* for dinner. Core members and assistants were seated around the large dinner table, with Jean at the far end. Meals at L'Arche are often loud affairs with sudden bursts of laughter and lots of singing. In the midst of the noise, the core member who was sitting next to me started gently stroking one of the braces that I wear. These medical devices extend from my knuckles to just below my elbows. I waited for any of the familiar questions: "What's wrong with you?" "What did you do?" "Carpal tunnel? I've had that!" "Skiing?" "When do you get them off?" No. As he continued to tap gently he leaned closer and said, very quietly in French: "That must be very painful. I will pray for you."

As Henri reminds us, visiting any L'Arche community draws you into an experience of its moment-to-moment life. It's happening right there, all around you, and isn't going to stop for a few minutes in order for you to try and find your bearings. This observer stance of the abled is so hard to overcome. I want to name and analyze what's going on, often overlooking the fact that I am in the middle of something unfolding at that very moment. Regardless of how able they might be to express it verbally, the week I was there, those core members were saying in their own way, "Welcome, stranger! You, being here, is important to me and to us." That little moment over dinner, well over a decade ago now, surfaced years of conditioned responses and reminded me of the ease with which I can fall into seeing some people as poor souls. As Henri learned from Adam Arnett, when you look beyond a handicap you discover the person that your ability filters mask. That night I remember feeling helpless and hopeless, and then I got over myself, passed the salad, and said, "*Merçi.*"

NINE: BE LOVED

I want Henri to have the last word, so I'll start with my conclusion. Like him, I have some unfinished flying and catching business to attend to.

In 1994, at a L'Arche gathering in a church in Mobile, Alabama, an exhausted Henri Nouwen said this to the packed crowd:

> One day, I was sitting in the caravan with Rodleigh, and Rodleigh said, "Henri, let me tell you something. I am the flyer and I make all these triples, you know. I go up the pedestal up to my bar and I let go of the bar and everybody applauds. But you know the real hero? Who the real hero is? The catcher."
>
> The catcher is the one on the flying catch-bar, going back and forth, and bam! He pulls him right up into the cupola of the circus. And Rodleigh said, "Henri, the greatest temptation for me is to try and catch the catcher. If I go there and say, 'Where are you?' then we will break each other's wrists. I have to make my triple and go down this way: my eyes closed, knowing that the catcher will be there to pull me right up into the cupola of the circus tent. Up! I know that I have to trust the catcher."
>
> Dear friends, we are called to do a lot of flying. You and I are called to do a lot of triples, and a lot of jumps, taking a lot of risks. Finally, you have to say: "Lord, into your hands I commend my spirit," and trust, that when it really comes down to it, He will really be there and pull you right up.

...And underneath is a very soft voice, a gentle voice, that says: "You. Are. My. Beloved. On you, my favor rests."

That's the voice that Jesus heard and that's the voice that you and I have to hear in the midst of all this shouting of other voices. You and I have to believe that you and I are the beloved sons and daughters of God, that you have been loved before your mother or father or sister or brother or church, or anyone loved you. And wounded you. Because no human being can love another human being without wounding them, too.

Your pain comes from the people who love you: your mother, your father, your priests, your church, your ministers. But underneath that pain there is a voice that says, "I have loved you with an everlasting love, before you were born, and I will love you after you die. I have loved you with an everlasting love. You are my beloved. You are my beloved daughter, you are my beloved son, from all eternity to all eternity. All the love that comes from your father and your mother and your sister, is only a reflection and a refraction that was there, even before you were born."[20]

This work has roots in radio. The documentary *Genius Born of Anguish: The Life and Legacy of Henri Nouwen* then became a book published by Paulist Press in the United States and by Novalis in Canada. As anyone in publishing knows, when no one is looking, books reproduce. This work is the firstborn of *Genius Born of Anguish*, and although we rarely know the impact of our work, we always know whom we should thank for their help in its creation. First, thanks to all the people who agreed to be interviewed for the radio documentary, and especially the smaller group included in this book: Nathan Ball, Robert Beloin, Jurjen Beumer, Bill Clarke, Christopher De Bono, Gabrielle Earnshaw, Robert Ellsberg, David Hagel, Robert A. Jonas, Sue Mosteller, Peter Naus, Laurent Nouwen, David Perrin, Ron Rolheiser, Richard Sipe, Rodleigh Stevens, Jean Vanier, and Carolyn Whitney Brown.

All writers need libraries and their ever-patient librarians. Special thanks to the Rosemount branch of the Ottawa Public Library, the Allie Library at Saint Paul University, the Morisset Library at the University of Ottawa, the Robards Library at the University of Toronto, the Toronto Metro Reference Library, and Library and Archives Canada. Thanks to Ken Puley at CBC Archives, and most of all, Gabrielle Earnshaw at the John M. Kelly Library at the University of St. Michael's College in the University of Toronto, without whose assistance this book would not have been completed.

The wellbeing of Henri Nouwen's published work is in the capable hands of Sally Keefe Cohen, Literary Manager of the

Henri Nouwen Legacy Trust and Karen Pascal, its Executive Director. The trust approved the use of all the excerpts from Henri's published works with permissions from the following publishers: Crossroad Publishing Company for *Life of the Beloved*, *Beyond the Mirror*, and *Our Second Birth*; HarperCollins for *Letters to Marc About Jesus: Living a Spiritual Life in a Material World*, and *Gracias: A Latin American Journal*; Ave Maria Press for *Can You Drink this Cup* and *In Memoriam*, now included in *A Sorrow Shared*; Penguin Random House for *Clowning in Rome: Reflections on Solitude, Prayer, and Contemplation*, *The Genesee Diary: Report From A Trappist Monastery*, *Home Tonight: Further Reflections on the Parable of the Prodigal Son*, *The Inner Voice of Love: A Journey Through Anguish to Freedom*, *Lifesigns: Intimacy, Fecundity, and Ecstasy in Christian Perspective*, *Reaching Out*, *The Return of the Prodigal Son*, and *The Wounded Healer*; and Orbis for *Adam: God's Beloved*, *Henri Nouwen: Selected Writings*, *Love in a Fearful Land: A Guatemala Story*, and *With Burning Hearts*.

Thanks, finally, to Denis de Klerck of Mansfield Press for permission to quote from the poetry of Pier Giorgio di Cicco.

Thanks also to all those authors who have ever written about Henri, and especially Michael W. Higgins, a rare and nurturing colleague whose boundless enthusiasm and comprehensive knowledge of the Catholic world is never short of astounding. After several collaborative projects, I thank him for giving me the encouragement to go solo on this book. Bernie Lucht of CBC Radio's *Ideas* continues to be a formidable presence in my professional life with his probing questions, insightful comments, and great lunches. His colleague, Dave Field, one of CBC's great sound engineers, taught me how to listen to more than one thing at once.

Early in my publishing career, I met Christopher De Bono at

an Ottawa conference about spirituality and mental health. Our paths crossed a few years later when I learned about his doctoral research into Henri's work on Anton Boisen. Now a good friend, Dr. De Bono's interview was pivotal to the series and to this book. Thanks to Heather Reid, whose downsizing resulted in her gift of rare Nouwen and Merton titles now in my personal library. Thanks to Jonathan Montaldo for nudges and encouragement from a distance over the years, and to S. T. (Steve) Georgiou for his loyal friendship and reminders that it was finally time for his editor to write something. Sue Mosteller and Robert Ellsberg helped to steer me away from some creative excursions from actuality. But no one in this entire list shares any responsibility for any errors. Those will be mine. Finally, thank you, Jon Sweeney, for your confidence in me and for your focused encouragement at every stage in the development of this book.

Ottawa, January 24, 2016. The Feast of St Francis de Sales, Doctor of the Church, and, since 1923, the patron saint of writers. And also the birthday of a friend.

The following people are quoted in the chapters of this book: Nathan Ball, Robert Beloin, Jurjen Beumer, Bill Clarke, Christopher De Bono, Gabrielle Earnshaw, Robert Ellsberg, Margaret Farley, David Hagel, Robert A. Jonas, Sue Mosteller, Peter Naus, Laurent Nouwen, David Perrin, Ron Rolheiser, Richard Sipe, Rodleigh Stevens, Jean Vanier, and Carolyn Whitney-Brown. Quotations from these participants are taken from their interview transcripts and will not have individual endnotes. All other published material is identified in endnotes.

EPIGRAPH

1. Henri Nouwen, *Letters to Marc: Living a Spiritual Life in a Material World* (New York: Harper and Row, 1987), 74.

INTRODUCTION

1. Michael Holroyd, "Our Friends the Dead," *The Guardian*, June 1, 2002, http://www.theguardian.com/books/2002/jun/01/featuresreviews. guardianreview36.

2. Julian Barnes, *Flaubert's Parrot* (London: Jonathan Cape, 1984), 38.

3. Hermione Lee, *Biography: A Very Short Introduction* (Oxford, UK: Oxford University Press, 2009), 93.

4. Leon Edel, *Writing Lives: Principia Biographica* (New York: Norton, 1984), 43.

5. Michael Holroyd, *Works on Paper: The Craft of Biography and Autobiography* (New York: Little, Brown, 2002), 4.

6. Nigel Hamilton, *How to Do Biography* (Cambridge, MA: Harvard University Press, 2008), 184.

7. Hermione Lee, *Virginia Woolf's Nose: Essays in Biography* (Princeton, NJ: Princeton University Press, 2005), 5.

8. Mary Carruthers, *The Craft of Thought: Meditation, Rhetoric, and the Making of Images, 400–1200* (Cambridge, UK: Cambridge University Press, 1998), 35.

9. Carruthers, 35.

10. Pope Francis, "Communication and Mercy," Message for the Fiftieth World Day of Social Communications, May 8, 2016. The message was signed by Pope Francis on Sunday, January 24, 2016, the feast of St. Francis de Sales, patron of journalists. Henri would have celebrated his eighty-fourth birthday that day.

11. Nouwen, *Letters to Marc*, 81.

12. This is the first excerpt from one of the interviews carried out in preparation for the documentary for CBC Radio. As noted above, this book includes excerpts from a smaller selection of that set of interviews.

13. Henri Nouwen, ¡Gracias! A Latin American Journal (New York: Harper and Row, 1982), 105.

14. Henri Nouwen, Life of the Beloved: Spiritual Living in a Secular World (New York: Crossroad, 1992), 26.

15. The Investigative Staff of the Boston Globe, Betrayal: The Crisis in the Catholic Church (New York: Little, Brown, 2012), 6.

16. Kevin Bazzana, Wondrous Strange: The Life and Art of Glenn Gould (Toronto: McClelland & Stewart, 2003), 2–6.

17. Bazzana, 10–11.

18. Bazzana, 48.

19. Henri Nouwen, The Genesee Diary (New York: Doubleday/Image, 1989), 207.

20. George Eliot, Middlemarch (Harmondsworth, UK: Penguin, 1994), 832.

21. Søren Kierkegaard, Fear and Trembling, trans. Walter Lowrie (Princeton, NJ: Princeton University Press, 1941), 218.

22. Holroyd, Works on Paper, 31–22.

CHAPTER ONE

1. Robert Ellsberg uses this line in The Saints' Guide to Happiness (New York: Farrar, Straus and Giroux, 2003), 166. He's describing a lecture that Henri gave at Yale in which he says these words while drawing a line across the full width of a chalkboard. This extended line replaced a shorter one, marked "1932" at one end and "2010?" at the other. Henri erased the question mark.

2. Tracy Kasaboski and Kristen den Hartog, The Occupied Garden: Recovering the Story of a Family in the War-Torn Netherlands (Toronto: McClelland & Stewart, 2008), 38.

3. Kasaboski and Hartog, 152–153.

4. Kasaboski and Hartog, 100.

5. Nouwen, Letters to Marc About Jesus, 13.

6. Nouwen, Genesee Diary, 93–94.

7. Henri Nouwen, Here and Now: Living in the Spirit (New York: Crossroad, 1994), 62.

8. Nouwen, Here and Now, 63.

9. Jurjen Beumer, Henri Nouwen: A Restless Seeking for God (New York: Crossroad, 1997), 23.

10. Anne Frank, The Diary of a Young Girl, trans. Susan Massotty (London: Folio Society, 2005), 52–53.

11. Etty Hillesum, *Etty: The Letters and Diaries of Etty Hillesum, 1941–1943*, ed. Klaas A. D. Smelik, trans., Arnold J. Pomerans (Grand Rapids: Eerdmans, 2002), 541.

12. Nouwen, *Here and Now*, 102.

13. Henri Nouwen, *Can You Drink The Cup?* (Notre Dame, IN: Ave Maria, 1996), 14.

14. Henri Nouwen, *Home Tonight: Further Reflections on the Parable of the Prodigal Son* (New York: Doubleday, 2009), xvi.

15. Peter Naus is chancellor emeritus of St. Jerome's University, Waterloo, Ontario. He taught psychology with a focus on human sexuality, and, later, gerontology, at the University of Notre Dame and then St. Jerome's University.

16. Anton Boisen, *Out of the Depths: An Autobiographical Study of Mental Disorder and Religious Experience* (New York: Harper and Brothers, 1960), 102.

17. Henri Nouwen, *The Wounded Healer* (New York: Doubleday, 1972), 86.

18. Henri Nouwen, *In Memoriam* (Notre Dame, IN: Ave Maria, 1980), 15.

19. Beth Porter, ed., *Befriending Life: Encounters with Henri Nouwen* (New York: Doubleday, 2002).

20. Nouwen, *Life of the Beloved*, 54.

21. Henri Nouwen, *Pray to Live, Thomas Merton: Contemplative Critic* (Montreal: Fides/Claretian, 1972), ix.

22. Thomas Merton, *The Journals of Thomas Merton*, vol. 6: *Learning to Love—1966–67*, ed. Christine M. Bochen (New York: Harper Collins, 1997), 231–232.

23. Henri attended that funeral in Atlanta and reported on it for the *National Catholic Reporter*.

24. Nouwen, *Pray to Live*, 37.

CHAPTER TWO

1. Beumer, 20.

2. Henri Nouwen, *Lifesigns: Intimacy, Fecundity, and Ecstasy in Christian Perspective* (New York: Image/Doubleday, 1986), 42.

3. Nouwen, *Pray to Live*, 55.

4. Henri Nouwen, *Intimacy* (Montreal: Fides/Dome, 1969), 36.

5. Nouwen, *Intimacy*, 138.

6. Nouwen, *Intimacy*, 52.

7. Nouwen, *Pray to Live*, 38.

8. Nouwen, *Pray to Live*, 38.

9. Nouwen, *Pray to Live*, 48

10. Nouwen, *Pray to Live*, 45.

11. In 1971 he published twice in Dutch: the book on Thomas Merton: *Bidden om het Leven: Het Contemplatief engagement van Thomas Merton* and the first version of "With Open Hands": *Met Open Handen: Notities over het Gebed.* Then, in 1987 came the first version of "Letters to Marc About Jesus": *Brieven aan Marc: over Jezus en de Zin van Het Leven.*

12. Carol Berry says she used Henri's notes for this course as she prepared *Vincent Van Gogh: His Spiritual Vision in Life and Art*, Modern Spiritual Master Series (Maryknoll, NY: Orbis, 2015).

13. Nouwen, *The Wounded Healer*, 33.

14. Nouwen, *The Wounded Healer*, 30.

15. Nouwen, *Genesee Diary*, 15.

16. Nouwen, *Genesee Diary*, 206.

17. Nouwen, *Genesee Diary*, 207.

18. Nouwen, *The Wounded Healer*, 89–90.

19. Henri Nouwen, *Reaching Out* (New York: Doubleday, 1975), 9.

20. Henri Nouwen, *Clowning in Rome: Reflections on Solitude, Celibacy, Prayer, and Contemplation* (New York: Image/Doubleday, 1979), 23.

21. Nouwen, *Clowning in Rome*, 95.

22. Nouwen, *Clowning in Rome*, 50.

23. According to Georgetown University's Center for Applied Research in the Apostolate, the number of ordinations, seminarians, religious sisters, religious brothers, all declined between 1965 and 1980, and even more so between 1995 to 2014. http://cara.georgetown.edu/frequently-requested-church-statistics/. KASKI is a research project in Religion and Society based in the Faculty of Philosophy, Theology, and Religion at Radboud Universiteit (Nijmegen). Their documentation (in Dutch only) charts an even more radical drop in numbers. See *De Rooms-Katholieke Kerk in Nederland 1960-1998*, Memorandum 317, March 2001, http://www.ru.nl/kaski/virtuele_map/publicaties/.

24. Nouwen, *Clowning in Rome*, 47–48.

25. Nouwen, *Here and Now*, 170.

26. Nouwen, *In Memoriam*, 13–14.

27. Nouwen, *In Memoriam*, 14.

28. Nouwen, *In Memoriam*, 56.

29. Nouwen, *In Memoriam*, 60.

30. Nouwen, *¡Gracias!*, xiv.

Chapter Three

1. *The Tablet*, October 10, 1910.

2. These details are included in the history and archive pages of the Maryknoll website, http://www.maryknoll.org/.

3. Nouwen, *Reaching Out*, 106.
4. Nouwen, *¡Gracias!*, 74.
5. The Canadian Conference of Catholic Bishops in their presentation to the UN's Special Session on Disarmament (February 16, 1982) summarized the situation this way: "In the last decade, we witnessed a dramatic rise in the number of military states, particularly in Third World Countries. In Latin America some twenty countries are governed by military or authoritarian regimes. In such Third World situations, increasing economic disparities and social injustices give rise to greater unrest for social change which, in turn, leads to a military takeover of the government in order to protect the *status quo* from the people. The military junta concentrates political power in its own hands and assumes control over the legislative body—directly or indirectly. Constitutional guarantees—democracy, free speech, free assembly, trade union rights, and even religious freedom—are often suspended or curtailed. Arbitrary detentions, torture of political prisoners, along with murder and assassination of opposition groups become commonplace." From *Do Justice!—The Social Teaching of the Canadian Catholic Bishops*, ed. E.F. Sheridan, SJ (Montreal: Éditions Paulines & The Jesuit Centre for Social Faith and Justice, 1987), 382–383.
6. Nouwen, *¡Gracias!*, 4.
7. Nouwen, *¡Gracias!*, 2.
8. Henri Nouwen, *Love in a Fearful Land—A Guatemala Story* (1985; Maryknoll, NY: Orbis 2006), 108.
9. Nouwen, *¡Gracias!*, 74.
10. Nouwen, *¡Gracias!*, 138.
11. Nouwen, *¡Gracias!*, 145.
12. Leonard Bernstein and Stephen Schwartz, *Mass*, CD libretto, (1971; New York: Sony Classical, 1997).
13. Bernstein and Schwartz.
14. Nouwen, *¡Gracias!*, 18.
15. Nouwen, *Life of the Beloved*, 102–103.
16. Humphrey Burton, *Leonard Bernstein* (London: Faber and Faber, 1994), 408.
17. Burton, 409.
18. *The Leonard Bernstein Archive*, http://www.leonardbernstein.com/mass_letters.htm.
19. Nouwen, *¡Gracias!*, 131.
20. Nouwen, *¡Gracias!*, 119.
21. Madeline M. Dorsey, MM, "Remembering the martyrs 30 years later,"

Maryknoll Magazine 201 (2010) http://www.maryknollmagazine.org/index.
php/magazines/201-remembering-the-martyrs-30-years-later.

22. Nouwen, *¡Gracias!*, 63.

23. Nouwen, *¡Gracias!*, 31.

24. Quoted by Robert Coles in his introduction to William Carlos Williams, *The Doctor Stories* (New York: New Directions, 1984), xiii (emphasis in original).

25. Nouwen, *¡Gracias!*, 148–149 (my emphasis).

26. Under Canada's system of a constitutional monarchy and parliamentary democracy, the Governor General is the appointed representative of the British monarch in Canada.

27. L'Arche website, http://www.larche.org/discover/ourhistory/.

28. Jean Vanier, *Life's Great Questions* (Cincinnati: Franciscan Media, 2015), 8.

29. Nouwen, *¡Gracias!*, 185.

30. *Honey and Salt: Selected Spiritual Writings of Saint Bernard of Clairvaux*, eds. John F. Thornton and Susan B. Varenne (New York: Vintage Spiritual Classics, 2007), 159.

31. For a more detailed explanation of the Nouwen/Ellsberg writer/editor relationship see "Editing Henri," Robert Ellsberg's contribution to *Remembering Henri : The Life and Legacy of Henri Nouwen*, eds. Gerald S. Twomey and Claude Pomerleau (Maryknoll, NY: Orbis, 2006), 59–66.

32. Robert A. Jonas has written very movingly about these circumstances in his book *Rebecca: A Father's Journey from Grief to Gratitude* (New York: Crossroad, 1996), and also in his introduction to the Modern Spiritual Masters Series anthology, *Henri Nouwen: Writings Selected with an Introduction by Robert A. Jonas* (Maryknoll, NY: Orbis, 2001).

33. Henri Nouwen, *The Inner Voice of Love: A Journey Through Anguish to Freedom* (New York: Image/Doubleday, 1996), 33.

34. Nouwen, *Home Tonight*, 13.

35. Letter to Theo van Gogh, The Hague, on or about Tuesday, May 16, 1882, in *Vincent van Gogh: The Letters*, ed. Leo Jansen, Hans Luijten, Nienke Bakker (Amsterdam; The Hague: Van Gogh Museum; Huygens ING, 2009).

36. Letter to Theo van Gogh, The Hague, Thursday and Friday, June 1–2, 1882, *Vincent van Gogh: The Letters*.

37. Letter to Theo van Gogh, The Hague, Thursday, July 6, 1882, *Vincent van Gogh: The Letters*.

38. Dr. J. Mundy, "The Gheel Question," *The Medical Critic* (July 1861), 10.

39. Mundy, 14. Although Mundy uses "Gheel," other citations use "Geel." To avoid confusion, except for this citation, I've used "Geel" as the Belgians do.

40. Richard P. McBrien, *Lives of the Saints* (New York: HarperCollins, 2001), 220.

41. David Farmer, *The Oxford Dictionary of Saints* (Oxford, UK: Oxford University Press, 1997) 145; and Karin Wells, "Psychiatric Community Care: Belgian Town Sets Gold Standard," CBC News, March 9, 2014. http://www.cbc.ca/news/world/psychiatric-community-care-belgian-town-sets-gold-standard-1.2557698.

42. Berry, ix.

43. Nouwen, *Love in a Fearful Land*, 99.

44. Nouwen, *Love in a Fearful Land*, 20.

45. Nouwen, *Lifesigns*, 93.

46. Nouwen, *Love in a Fearful Land* 102.

47. Nouwen, *Lifesigns*, 63.

48. Nouwen, *Lifesigns*, 64.

49. Amnesty International, "The Task of Reading Guatemala's Bones," Amnesty International News Service, November 15, 2012, https://www.amnesty.org/en/latest/news/2012/11/task-reading-guatemala-s-bones/.

50. Nouwen, *Love in a Fearful Land*, 122. Fr. John Vesey eventually moved to China as a Maryknoll associate and worked there for a decade before returning to diocesan work in Brooklyn in 2012.

51. Dr. David B. Perrin now teaches religious studies at St. Jerome's University in Waterloo, Ontario. He is also the author of *Studying Christian Spirituality* (New York: Routledge, 2007).

CHAPTER FOUR

1. Nouwen, *Lifesigns*, 50.

2. L'Arche website, http://www.larche.org.

3. Ian Brown: "Jean Vanier's Comfort and Joy: What we have to do is find places of hope," *The Globe and Mail*, December 19, 2015.

4. Henri Nouwen, *Beyond the Mirror* (New York: Crossroad, 1990), 28.

5. Henri Nouwen, *Adam: God's Beloved* (Maryknoll, NY: Orbis, 1997), 42, 45.

6. Nouwen, *Adam*, 48, 51.

7. Nouwen, *Life of the Beloved*, 99

8. Andrew Solomon, *The Noonday Demon: An Atlas of Depression* (New York: Simon and Schuster, 2001), 62–63.

9. Nouwen, *Home Tonight*, 33.

10. Nouwen, *Life of the Beloved*, 32.

11. James Hillman, *Blue Fire: Selected Writings by James Hillman*, ed. Thomas Moore (New York: Harper and Row, 1989), 153.

12. Solomon, 48.

13. Nouwen, *The Inner Voice of Love*, 5.

14. Nouwen, *The Inner Voice of Love*, 30.
15. Nouwen, *The Inner Voice of Love*, 50.
16. Nouwen, *The Inner Voice of Love*, 110.
17. Henri Nouwen, *The Return of the Prodigal Son* (New York: Image/ Doubleday, 1994), 13.

CHAPTER FIVE

1. Henri Nouwen, *Our Second Birth* (1998; New York: Crossroad 2006), 74.
2. *Vader en zoon* is Dutch for "father and son."
3. Nouwen, *Our Second Birth*, 78.
4. This smiling grace-filled moment of Henri bouncing in the safety net was recreated in the documentary film *Angels Over the Net*, originally produced as an episode in the series *Overal et Nergens* (*All Over the Place*) for Netherlands television and aired there in 1995.
5. Nouwen, *Clowning in Rome*, 104.
6. Nouwen, *Clowning in Rome*, 109.
7. Nouwen, *Adam*, 97.
8. Nouwen, *Adam*, 98.
9. Nouwen, *Adam*, 90.
10. Nouwen, *Adam*, 127–128.

CHAPTER SIX

1. *Yale Faculty Handbook*, 2015 Edition, 123. http://provost.yale.edu/sites/default/files/files/Faculty%20Handbook_9-18-15.pdf.
2. Harvard University, *General Leave Policy*, 2015, http://academic-appointments.fas.harvard.edu/general-leave-policies.
3. Nouwen, *Our Second Birth*, 11.
4. Nouwen, *Our Second Birth*, 71.
5. Nouwen, *Here and Now*, 157
6. Nouwen, *Our Second Birth*, 98.
7. The Hermitage website contains an interactive webpage that takes you, virtually, inside room 254, the celebrated "Rembrandt Room." https://www.hermitagemuseum.org/wps/portal/hermitage/explore/buildings/locations/room/B40_F2_H254/?lng=en.
8. Jakob Rosenberg, *Rembrandt: Life and Work* (Ithaca, NY: Cornell University Press, 1948), 232, 234.
9. Rosenberg, 230.
10. Rosenberg, 234.
11. Simon Schama, *The Embarrassment of Riches: An Interpretation of Dutch Culture in the Golden Age* (London: William Collins, 1987), 122.

12. Nouwen, *The Return of the Prodigal Son*, 127.
13. Nouwen, *The Return of the Prodigal Son*, 15.
14. Nouwen, *The Return of the Prodigal Son*, 117.
15. Nouwen, *The Return of the Prodigal Son*, 139.
16. Nouwen, *Our Second Birth*, 30.
17. Michelle O'Rourke, *Befriending Death: Henri Nouwen and a Spirituality of Dying* (Maryknoll, NY: Orbis, 2009), xv.

CHAPTER SEVEN

1. Sue Mosteller, a Sister of St. Joseph, who in addition to compiling unfinished works of Henri's is also an accomplished author. Her own books include *My Brother, My Sister* (about Jean Vanier and Mother Teresa) (Mahwah, NJ: Paulist, 1972); *Body Broken, Body Blessed: Reflections from Life in Community* (Ottawa: Novalis, 1996); and *Light Through the Crack: Life After Loss* (New York: Image Books/Doubleday, 2006).
2. Jean Vanier, *Our Lives Together: A Memoir in Letters* (Toronto: HarperCollins, 2007), 370.
3. Nouwen, *The Return of the Prodigal Son*, 69–70.
4. Ronald Rolheiser, *The Holy Longing: The Search for a Christian Spirituality* (New York: Doubleday, 1999), 240.
5. Michael Swan, "Famous Catholic Author Nouwen Moved to Anglican Cemetery," *The Catholic Register*, November 25, 2010, http://www.catholicregister.org/item/9400-famous-catholic-author-nouwen-moved-to-anglican-cemetery.
6. Henri Nouwen, quoted by Michelle O'Rourke in *Befriending Death*, 93.

AFTERWORD

1. "Stalking the Holy: The Politics of Saint Making" aired on CBC Radio's *Ideas with Paul Kennedy* in 2006.
2. Nouwen, *Our Second Birth*, 30.
3. Abraham Joshua Heschel, *Man Is Not Alone: A Philosophy of Religion* (New York: Farrar, Straus and Giroux, 1951), 162.
4. St. Werburgh (circa 650–702) is the patron saint of Chester (UK), where I was born. A princess, she is one of many royal saints in the family that ruled Mercia (the middle bit of England), a kingdom long before the Norman Conquest and before England became Britain. The geese at her feet relate to a miracle in a life where "legend and guesswork have had free scope." See James Tait, ed., *The Chartulary or Register of the Abbey of Werburgh* (Manchester, UK: The Chetham Society, 1923). Around 900, her remains were moved northwest to Chester for safety from advancing Danes and later

enshrined inside the Benedictine abbey founded there in 1092. In 1542, the Reformation rebranded St. Werburgh's Abbey as the Cathedral of Christ and the Blessed Virgin. Disassembled rather than destroyed, her shrine escaped the damage suffered by many other monasteries and churches. Reassembled with lots of bits missing, it stands at the rear of the cathedral's Lady Chapel.

5. Thomas Merton, *New Seeds of Contemplation* (New York: New Directions, 1961), 31.

6. Ellsberg, xvii. The movement for the formal canonization of Dorothy Day was supported by the late Cardinal Edward Egan (like Henri, born in 1932) through the Dorothy Day Guild, an association set up by the Archdiocese of New York. http://dorothydayguild.org/.

7. O'Rourke, 106.

8. Vanier, *Life's Great Questions*, 2.

9. Bernie Lucht, ed., *Ideas: Brilliant Thinkers Speak Their Minds* (Fredericton, NB: Goose Lane, 2005), 11.

10. Merton, *New Seeds of Contemplation*, 32 (emphasis in original).

11. Eliot, 838.

12. Carolyn Whitney-Brown, quoted by Michael Ford in *Wounded Prophet: A Portrait of Henri J.M. Nouwen* (New York: Image/Doubleday, 1999), xv; and for more of her insights into Henri's Daybreak years see her "Celebration and Hardwork" in *Remembering Henri*, 119–137.

13. Thornton Wilder, *Our Town*, in *Collected Plays & Writings on Theater* (New York: The Library of America, 2007), 207.

14. Marilynne Robinson, *The Givenness of Things* (New York: HarperCollins, 2015), 286.

15. Bernard of Clairvaux, *Honey and Salt*, 156.

16. Robert Frost, "The Road Not Taken," in *The Poetry of Robert Frost* (New York: Henry Holt, 1969), 105.

17. Pier Giorgio Di Cicco, "Desert Song 2," in *The Dark Time of Angels* (Toronto: Mansfield, 2003), 80.

18. David Hagel, "Ideas at 50, Part 1," *Ideas with Paul Kennedy*, CBC Radio One and Sirius Satellite Radio, October 9, 2015, http://www.cbc.ca/radio/ideas/ideas-at-50-part-1-1.3259156.

19. Jean Vanier, *Drawn into the Mystery of Jesus Through the Gospel of John* (Ottawa: Novalis, 2004).

20. Henri J.M. Nouwen, *Finding Our Sacred Center: An Evening with Henri Nouwen:* L'Arche produced video recording of presentation at Dauphin Way United Methodist Church, Mobile, Alabama, May 5, 1994; V34, Box 331, Henri Nouwen Archives. Edited and transcribed by the author.

Amnesty International. "The Task of Reading Guatemala's Bones," Amnesty International News Service, November 15, 2012. https://www.amnesty.org/en/latest/news/2012/11/task-reading-guatemala-s-bones/.

L'Arche International. Website, http://www.larche.org.

Barnes, Julian. *Flaubert's Parrot.* London: Jonathan Cape, 1984.

Bazzana, Kevin. *Wondrous Strange: The Life and Art of Glenn Gould.* Toronto: McClelland & Stewart, 2003.

St. Bernard of Clairvaux. *Honey and Salt: Selected Spiritual Writings of Saint Bernard of Clairvaux.* Edited by John F. Thornton and Susan B. Varenne. New York: Vintage Spiritual Classics, 2007.

Bernstein, Leonard, with Stephen Schwartz. *Mass.* New York: Sony Classical, 1971 and 1997.

Berry, Carol. *Vincent Van Gogh: His Spiritual Vision in Life and Art.* Maryknoll, NY: Orbis, 2015.

Beumer, Jurjen. *Henri Nouwen: A Restless Seeking for God.* New York: Crossroad, 1997.

Boisen, Anton T. *Out of the Depths: An Autobiographical Study of Mental Disorder and Religious Experience.* New York: Harper, 1960.

Brown, Ian. "Jean Vanier's Comfort and Joy: What We Have to Do Is Find Places of Hope," *The Globe and Mail,* December 19, 2015.

Burton, Humphrey. *Leonard Bernstein.* London: Faber and Faber, 1994.

Canadian Conference of Catholic Bishops. *Do Justice: The Social Teaching of the Canadian Catholic Bishops.* Edited by E.F. Sheridan, SJ. Montreal: Éditions Paulines & The Jesuit Centre for Social Faith and Justice, 1987.

CARA, Center for Applied Research in the Apostolate, Georgetown University.

Carruthers, Mary. *The Craft of Thought: Meditation, Rhetoric, and the Making of Images, 400–1200.* Cambridge, UK: Cambridge University Press, 1998.

Di Cicco, Pier Giorgio. *The Dark Time of Angels.* Toronto: Mansfield, 2003.

Earnshaw, Gabrielle. From *The Henri J.M. Nouwen Collection: An Introduction to the Nouwen Archive Published by the John M. Kelly Library.* Toronto: University of St. Michael's College, 2011.

Edel, Leon. *Writing Lives: Principia Biographica.* New York: Norton, 1984.

Eliot, George. *Middlemarch.* Harmondsworth, UK: Penguin, 1994.

Ellsberg, Robert. *The Saints' Guide to Happiness.* New York: Farrar, Straus and Giroux, 2003.

Farmer, David. *Oxford Dictionary of Saints.* Oxford, UK: Oxford University Press, 1997.

Ford, Michael. *Wounded Prophet: A Portrait of Henri J.M. Nouwen.* New York: Image, 1999.

Pope Francis. "Communication and Mercy," Message for the Fiftieth World Day of Social Communications, 2016, https://w2.vatican.va/content/francesco/en/messages/communications/documents/papa-francesco_20160124_messaggio-comunicazioni-sociali.html.

Frank, Anne. *The Diary of a Young Girl.* Translated by Susan Massotty. London: Folio Society, 2005.

Frost, Robert. *The Poetry of Robert Frost.* New York: Henry Holt, 1969.

Hagel, David. "Ideas at 50, Part 1," *Ideas with Paul Kennedy.* CBC Radio One and Sirius Satellite Radio, October 9, 2015, http://www.cbc.ca/radio/ideas/ideas-at-50-part-1-1.3259156.

Hamilton, Nigel. *How to Do Biography.* Cambridge, MA: Harvard University Press, 2008.

Heschel, Abraham Joshua. *Man Is Not Alone: A Philosophy of Religion.* New York: Farrar, Straus and Giroux, 1951.

Higgins, Michael W., and Kevin Burns, *Genius Born of Anguish: The Life and Legacy of Henri Nouwen.* Mahwah, NJ: Paulist, 2012.

———. *Genius Born of Anguish: The Life and Legacy of Henri Nouwen,* CBC Radio One and Sirius Satellite Radio, January 9, 16, and 23, 2013. http://www.cbc.ca/radio/ideas/genius-born-of-anguish-part-1-1.2913520; http://www.cbc.ca/radio/ideas/genius-born-of-anguish-part-2-1.2913526;

http://www.cbc.ca/radio/ideas/genius-born-of-anguish-part-3-1.2913533.

————. *Stalking the Holy: The Politics of Saint Making*, CBC Radio One, February and March, 2006. http://www.cbc.ca/radio/ideas/stalking-the-holy-revisited-1.2913890.

Hillesum, Etty. *Etty: The Letters and Diaries of Etty Hillesum, 1941–1943*. Edited by Klaas A.D. Smelik. Translated by Arnold J. Pomerans. Grand Rapids: Eerdmans, 2002.

Hillman, James. *Blue Fire: Selected Writings by James Hillman*. Edited by Thomas Moore. New York: Harper and Row, 1989.

Holroyd, Michael. *Works on Paper: The Craft of Biography and Autobiography*. New York: Little, Brown, 2002.

————. "Our Friends the Dead," *The Guardian*, May 31, 2002, http://www.theguardian.com/books/2002/jun/01/featuresreviews. guardianreview36.

The Investigative Staff of the *Boston Globe*. *Betrayal: The Crisis in the Catholic Church*. New York: Little, Brown, 2012.

Jonas, Robert A. *Rebecca: A Father's Journey from Grief to Gratitude*. New York: Crossroad, 1996.

Kasaboski, Tracy, and Kristen den Hartog. *The Occupied Garden: Recovering the Story of a Family in the War-Torn Netherlands*. Toronto: McClelland & Stewart, 2008.

KASKI – Faculty of Philosophy, Theology, and Religion, Radboud Universiteit. *De Rooms-Katholieke Kerk in Nederland 1960-1998*, Memorandum nr. 317, March 2001. Online documentation. http://www.ru.nl/kaski/virtuele_map/publicaties.

Lee, Hermione. *Biography: A Very Short Introduction*. Oxford, UK: Oxford University Press, 2009.

Lucht, Bernie, ed. *Ideas: Brilliant Thinkers Speak Their Minds*. Fredericton, NB: Goose Lane, 2005.

McBrien, Richard P. *Lives of the Saints*. New York: HarperCollins, 2001.

Merton, Thomas. *The Journals of Thomas Merton*, vol. 4: *Turning Toward the World*. Edited by Victor A. Kramer. New York: HarperSanFrancisco, 1997.

———. *The Journals of Thomas Merton*, Vol. 6: *Learning to Love*. Edited by Christine M. Bochen. New York: HarperCollins 1997.

———. *New Seeds of Contemplation*. New York: New Directions, 1961.

Mundy, J. "The Gheel Question," *The Medical Critic*, July 1861.

Nouwen, Henri J.M. *Adam: God's Beloved*. Maryknoll, NY: Orbis, 1997.

———. *Beyond the Mirror*. New York: Crossroad, 1990.

———. *Can You Drink the Cup?* Notre Dame, IN: Ave Maria, 1996.

———. *Clowning in Rome: Reflections on Solitude, Celibacy, Prayer, and Contemplation*. New York: Image/Doubleday, 1979.

———. *Encounters with Merton: Spiritual Reflections*. New York: Crossroad, 1981.

———. *Finding Our Sacred Center: An Evening with Henri Nouwen*. L'Arche video, 1994. V34, Box 331, Henri Nouwen Archives.

———. *The Genesee Diary: Report from a Trappist Monastery*. New York: Doubleday/Image, 1989.

———. *¡Gracias! A Latin American Journal*. New York: Harper and Row, 1982.

———. *Heart Speaks to Heart: Three Prayers to Jesus*. Notre Dame, IN: Ave Maria, 1989.

———. *Henri Nouwen: Writings Selected with an Introduction by Robert A. Jonas*. Maryknoll, NY: Orbis, 2001.

———. *Here and Now: Living in the Spirit*. New York: Crossroad, 1994.

———. *Home Tonight: Further Reflections on the Parable of the Prodigal Son*. New York: Doubleday, 2009.

———. *In Memoriam*. Notre Dame, IN: Ave Maria, 1980.

———. *In the Name of Jesus: Reflections of Christian Leadership*. New York: Crossroad, 1993.

———. *The Inner Voice of Love: A Journey Through Anguish to Freedom*. New York: Image/Doubleday, 1996.

———. *Intimacy*. Montreal: Fides/Dome, 1969.

———. *Letters to Marc: Living a Spiritual Life in a Material World*. New York: Harper and Row, 1987.

————. *Life of the Beloved: Spiritual Living in a Secular World*. New York: Crossroad, 1992.

————. *Lifesigns: Intimacy, Fecundity, and Ecstasy in Christian Perspective*. New York: Image Doubleday, 1986.

————. *Love in a Fearful Land: A Guatemala Story*. 1985. Maryknoll, NY: Orbis, 2006.

————. *Our Second Birth*. 1998. New York: Crossroad 2006.

————. *Peacework: Prayer, Resistance, Community*. Maryknoll, NY: Orbis, 2005.

————. *Pray to Live: Thomas Merton: Contemplative Critic*. Montreal: Fides/ Claretian, 1972.

————. *Reaching Out*. New York: Doubleday, 1975.

————. *The Return of the Prodigal Son*. New York: Image/Doubleday, 1994.

————. *A Sorrow Shared*. Notre Dame, IN: Ave Maria, 2010.

————. *With Burning Hearts: A Meditation on the Eucharistic Life*. Maryknoll, NY: Orbis, 1994.

————. *The Wounded Healer*. New York: Doubleday, 1972.

O'Rourke, Michelle. *Befriending Death: Henri Nouwen and a Spirituality of Dying*. Maryknoll, NY: Orbis, 2009.

Perrin, David B. *Studying Christian Spirituality*. New York: Routledge, 2007.

Porter, Beth, ed. *Befriending Life: Encounters with Henri Nouwen*. New York: Doubleday, 2002.

Robinson, Marilynne. *The Givenness of Things*. New York: HarperCollins, 2015.

Rolheiser, Ronald. *The Holy Longing: The Search for a Christian Spirituality*. New York: Doubleday, 1999.

Rosenberg, Jakob. *Rembrandt: Life and Work*. Ithaca, NY: Cornell University Press, 1948.

Schama, Simon. *The Embarrassment of Riches: An Interpretation of Dutch Culture in the Golden Age*. London: William Collins, 1987.

Solomon, Andrew. *The Noonday Demon: An Atlas of Depression*. New York: Simon and Schuster, 2001.

Swan, Michael. "Famous Catholic Author Nouwen Moved to Anglican Cemetery," *The Catholic Register*, November 25, 2010.

"The Eucharistic Congress at Montreal," *The Tablet*, October 10, 1910.

Tait, James, ed. *The Chartulary or Register of the Abbey of Werburgh*. Manchester, UK: The Chetham Society, 1923.

Twomey, Gerald S., and Claude Pomerleau, eds. *Remembering Henri: The Life and Legacy of Henri Nouwen* (Maryknoll, NY: Orbis, 2006).

Vincent van Gogh: The Letters. Edited by Jansen, Leo, Hans Luijten, and Nienke Bakker. Amsterdam; The Hague: Van Gogh Museum; Huygens ING, 2009.

Vanier, Jean. *Drawn into the Mystery of Jesus Through the Gospel of John*. Ottawa: Novalis, 2004.

———. *Life's Great Questions*. Cincinnati: Franciscan Media, 2015.

———. *Our Lives Together: A Memoir in Letters*. Toronto: HarperCollins, 2007.

Wells, Karin. "Psychiatric Community Care: Belgian Town Sets Gold Standard." CBC Radio News Documentary, March 9, 2014. http://www.cbc.ca/news/worldpsychiatric-community-care-belgian-town-sets-gold-standard-1.2557698.

Wilder, Thornton. *Our Town*. In *Collected Plays & Writings on Theater*. New York: Library of America, 2007.

Williams, William Carlos. *The Doctor Stories*. New York: New Directions, 1984.

Excerpts from *Adam: God's Beloved* by Henri J.M. Nouwen. Copyright ©1997 by Orbis Books, P.O. Box 302, Maryknoll, NY 10545. Used with permission of the publisher.

Excerpts from *A Sorrow Shared: A Combined Edition of the Nouwen Classics "In Memoriam" and "A Letter of Consolation"* by Henri J.M. Nouwen. Copyright ©2010 by Ave Maria Press, Inc., P.O. Box 428, Notre Dame, IN 46556, www.avemariapress.com. Used with permission of the publisher.

Excerpts from *Beyond the Mirror* by Henri J.M. Nouwen. Copyright ©1990 by Crossroad Publishing Company, Inc., 831 Chestnut Ridge Road, Chestnut Ridge, NY 10977. Used with permission of the publisher.

Excerpts from *Can You Drink the Cup?* by Henri J.M. Nouwen. Copyright ©1996, 2006 by Ave Maria Press, Inc., P.O. Box 428, Notre Dame, IN 46556, www.avemariapress.com. Used with permission of the publisher.

Excerpts from *Clowning in Rome: Reflections on Solitude, Prayer, and Contemplation* by Henri J.M. Nouwen. Copyright ©1979 by Image/Doubleday, Penguin Random House group, 1745 Broadway, New York, NY 10019. Used with permission of the publisher.

Excerpts from *The Genesee Diary: Report From A Trappist Monastery* by Henri J.M. Nouwen. Copyright ©1989 by Image/Doubleday, Penguin Random House group, 1745 Broadway, New York, NY 10019. Used with permission of the publisher.

Excerpts from pages 13 and 74 of *Gracias!: A Latin American Journal* by Henri J.M. Nouwen. Copyright ©1982 by HarperCollins Publishers, 195 Broadway 24th Floor, New York, NY 10007. Used with permission of the publisher.

Excerpts from *Henri Nouwen: Writings Selected with an Introduction by Robert A. Jonas* by Henri J.M. Nouwen. Copyright ©2001 by Orbis Books, P.O. Box 302, Maryknoll, NY 10545. Used with permission of the publisher.

About the Author

Kevin Burns taught theater arts in a British high school before moving to Canada. He taught in the drama department of the University of Alberta and then became a radio producer for the Canadian Broadcasting Corporation. He was also an editor for Novalis, specializing in spirituality, religion, and theology. His radio documentaries for the CBC include the New York Festival's Gold Award–winning *Genius Born of Anguish: The Life and Legacy of Henri Nouwen.* The tie-in book, coauthored with Michael W. Higgins and published in 2013, received a Catholic Press Association of the United States and Canada award in the category of spirituality.